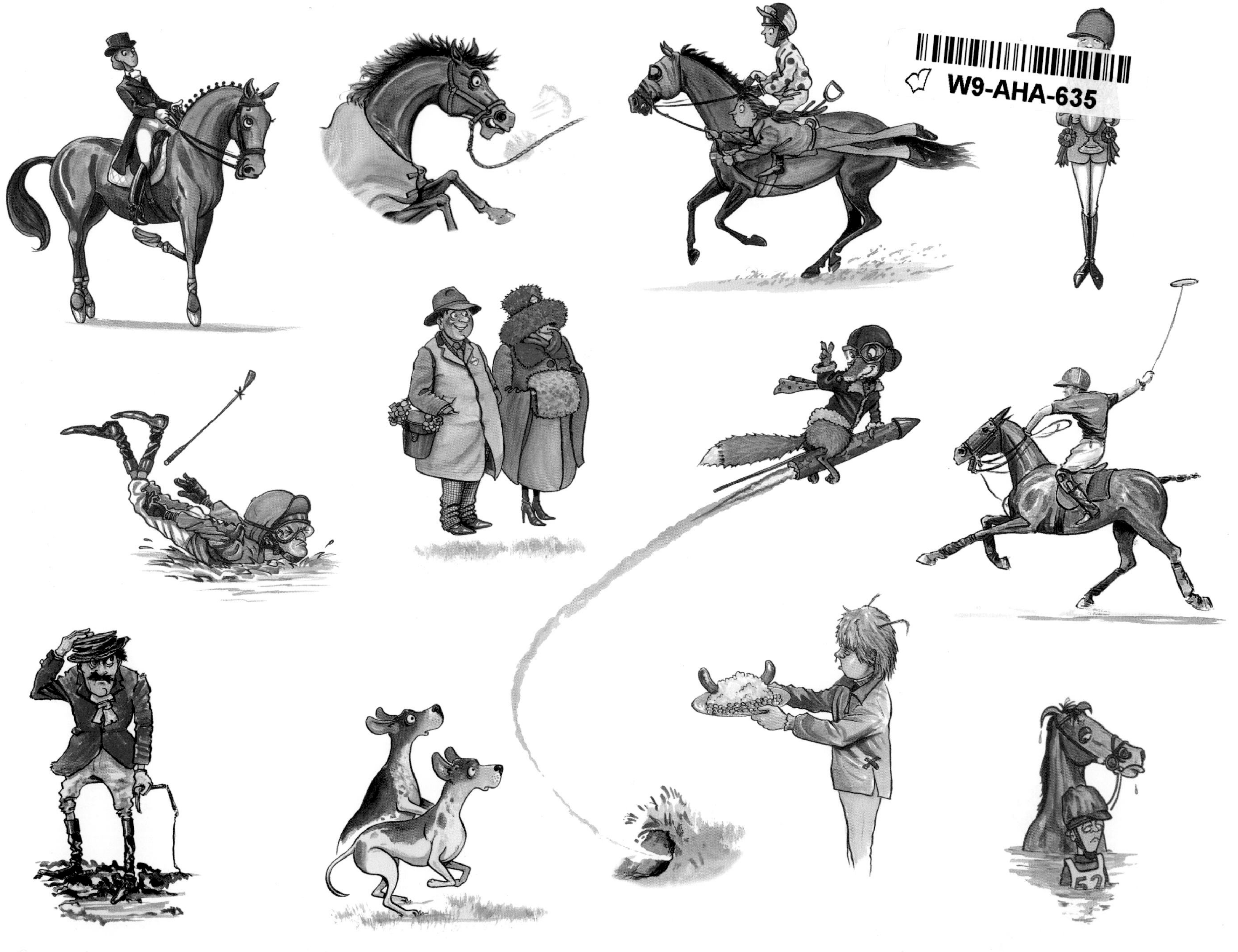
52

HORSES FOR COURSES

HORSES FOR COURSES

A short Horse Course by Bryn Parry
with *Horse Types* by Giles Catchpole

SWAN·HILL
PRESS

Horses for Courses
is dedicated to the memory
of Norman Thelwell,
the great cartoonist.

Copyright © 2004 Bryn Parry
© Giles Catchpole *Horse Types* text

First published in the UK in 2004
by Swan Hill Press, an imprint of Quiller Publishing Ltd

British Library Cataloguing-in-Publication Data
A catalogue record for this book is available from the British Library

ISBN 0 904057 44 6

Printed in Hong Kong

Swan Hill Press
An imprint of Quiller Publishing Ltd.
Wykey House, Wykey, Shrewsbury, SY4 1JA
Tel: 01939 261616 Fax: 01939 261606
E-mail: info@quillerbooks.com

Website: www.swanhillbooks.com

CONTENTS

Introduction

I do not ride. I had some lessons on Hercules at our local riding school and bounced around perfecting what I called the rising trot until his huge girth bent my knees into an unnatural shape and I gave up. A while later I was perched on an Appaloosa pony called Storm and wobbled up a canyon in the Idaho wilderness until I had very little skin left on my bottom. The depressing fact is, and anyone who has seen me on a horse will agree, that I do not ride.

I ought to be able to ride if breeding has anything to do with it; riding is in my blood, or should be. My Grandfather bred polo ponies in Pindi, my Grandmother hunted sidesaddle with the Peshawar Vale Hunt and my Mother, Aunt and Uncle all won their classes at numerous gymkhanas. Despite this very proper pedigree, I have never really taken to the saddle and so to think that I might fill a book with equestrian cartoons is probably an act of extreme folly.

Riding is the most wonderful subject for a cartoonist and I have really enjoyed painting horses and their riders. Emma and I have our trade stand at Burghley Horse Trials and I like to sneak out of the tent to watch the riders warming up in the collecting ring before their big dressage moment. They are totally focussed and so elegant, but I am afraid I see them wearing ballet shoes and tutus. When I go to the races, my mind goes into overdrive and I see parachutes on the jockeys' backs, or an ejector seat instead of a saddle. If I were a fox, I think that a spot of ambushing would be in order. The brain of a cartoonist must be very strange.

A great number of people have helped me with this book and I should thank them all by name. My problem is that if I name them, I will inevitably insult someone by omitting them or implicate them by their inclusion. People have been extremely kind and very patient when answering my questions. I have been to the races, nosed around yards, visited RDA lessons, frozen my assets at Point to Points, jogged over fields following the hunt and trod in my fair share of divots. People have told me about their favourite ponies and least favourite Types, and I have certainly met some of them; I hope that I have portrayed them accurately. You know who you are, so let me just say thank you so much for your advice, generosity and help; I could not have produced this without you.

I can and will name Giles Catchpole. Giles and I work together on our page in *The Shooting Gazette* and together we have produced various shooting books, with his words and my cartoons. He has very kindly agreed to write the twenty-one Horse Types that are dotted throughout the book. His contribution to *Horses for Courses* is vital, his style unique and I am very grateful for his wonderful witty words. Thank you, Giles.

The other person I will mention is Norman Thelwell. I went to see him at his riverside studio during the summer of 1986, shortly after I had begun my new life as a cartoonist. I remember the feeling of awe at meeting one of my heroes and someone who had made a career from cartooning. The meeting both inspired me and made me feel terribly aware of my limitations. I was finishing this book eighteen years later when I was saddened to read his obituary and so dedicate *Horses for Courses* to the creator of the Thelwell Pony; I hope he would have approved.

I think everyone who rides should be admired for their courage and dedication. I just hope that having read this book they will retain their sense of humour.

Bryn Parry

CONFORMATION

SET ON WELL

SET ON HIGH

SET ON LOW

12

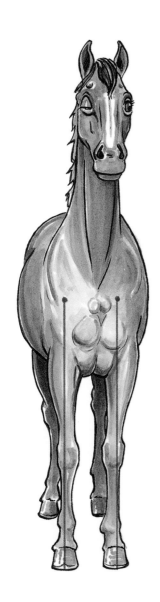

BOWLEGGED **COW HOCKED** **PIGEON TOED**

13

THE ASSISTED MOUNT

MOTIVATION

SEPARATION

IRRITATION

SITTING TROT

RISING TROT

VERY GOOD SEAT

TURNING ON THE FOREHAND

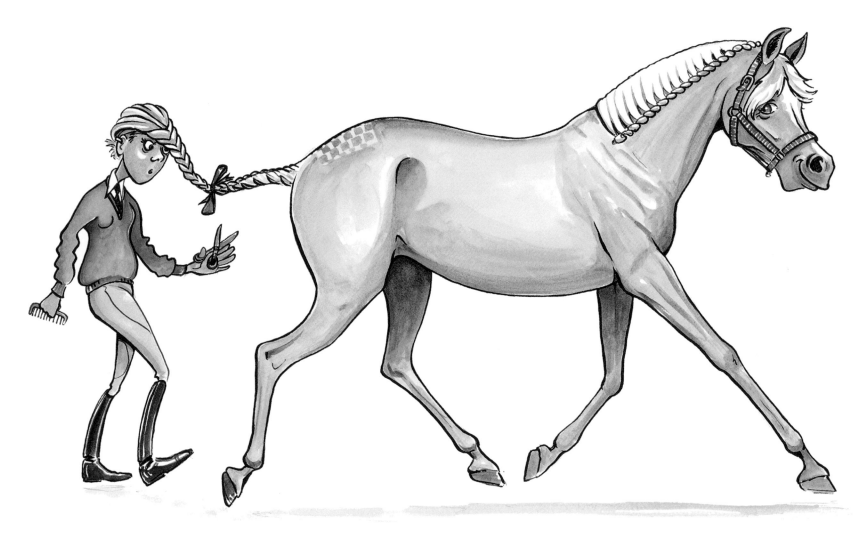

PLAITING

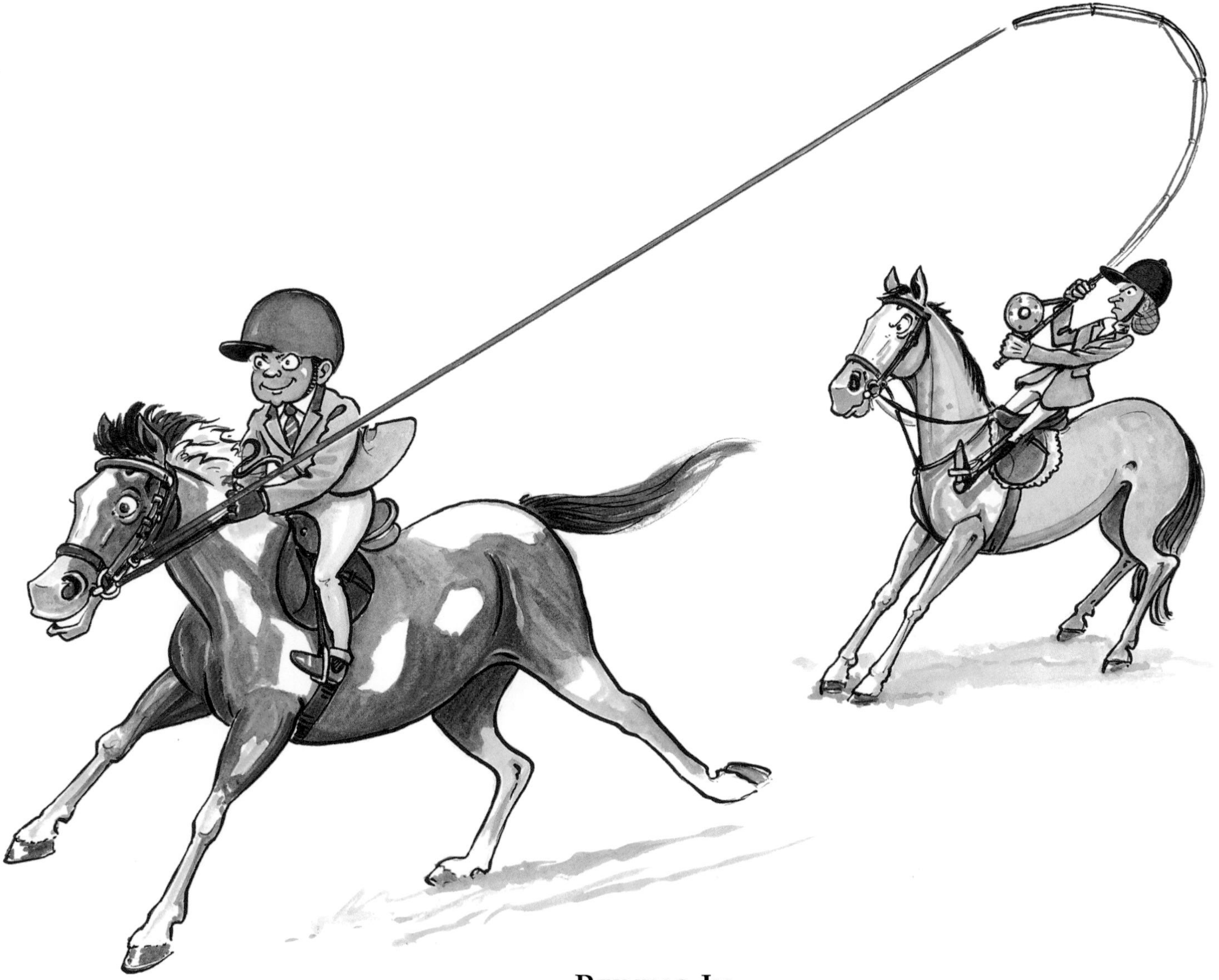

REINING IN

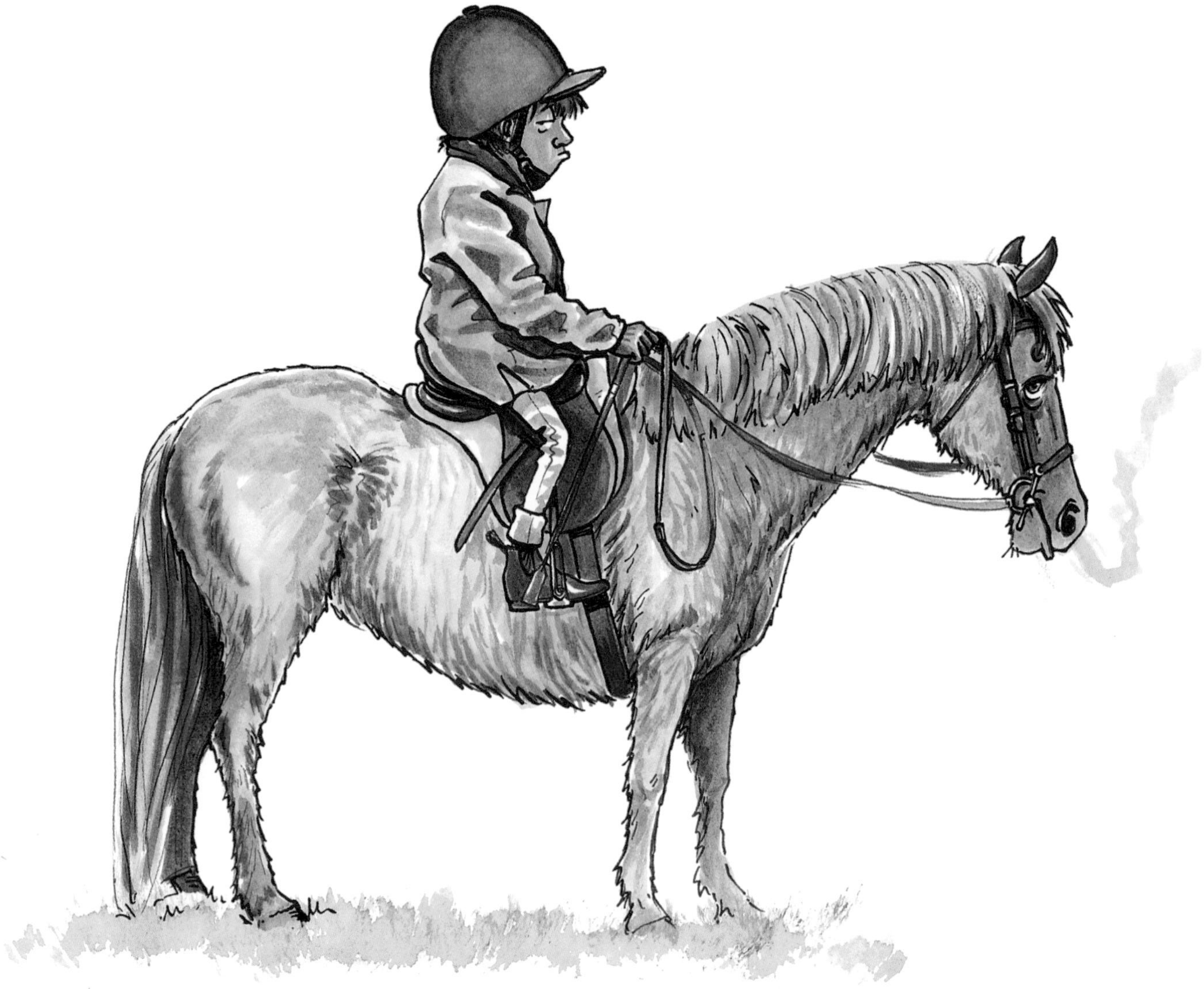

Hacked Off

PUNK PONY

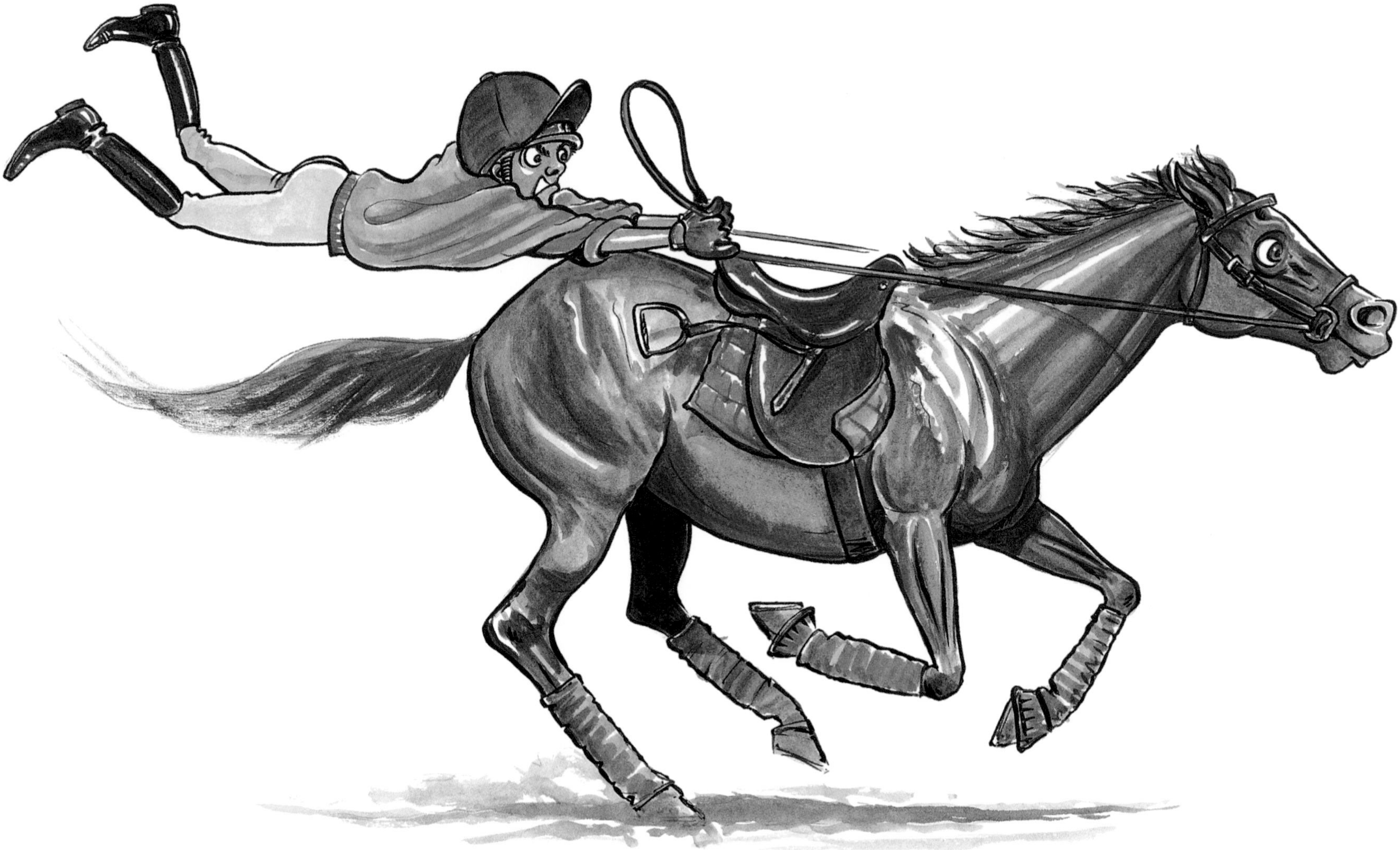

Getting a Grip

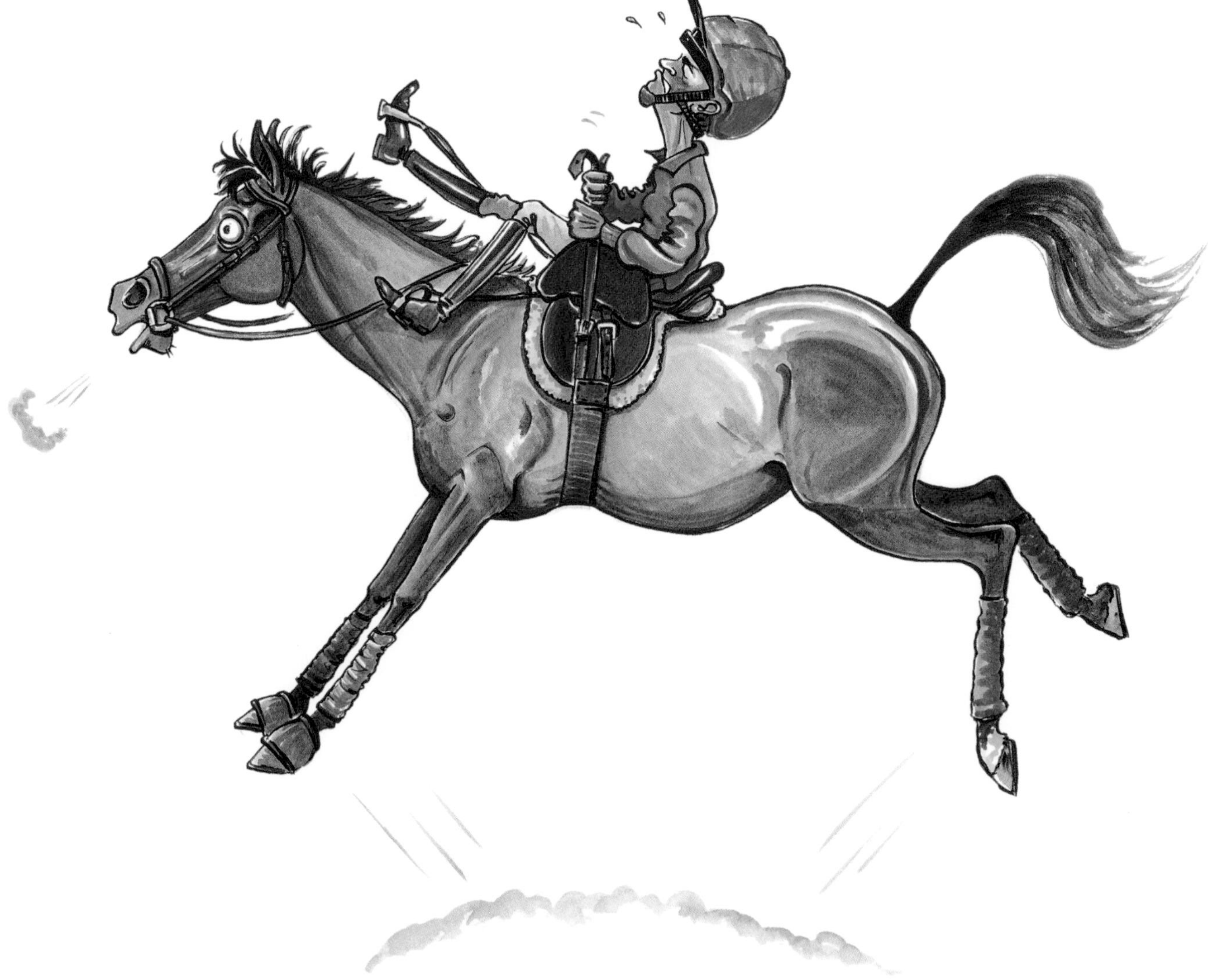

Tightening The Girth When Mounted

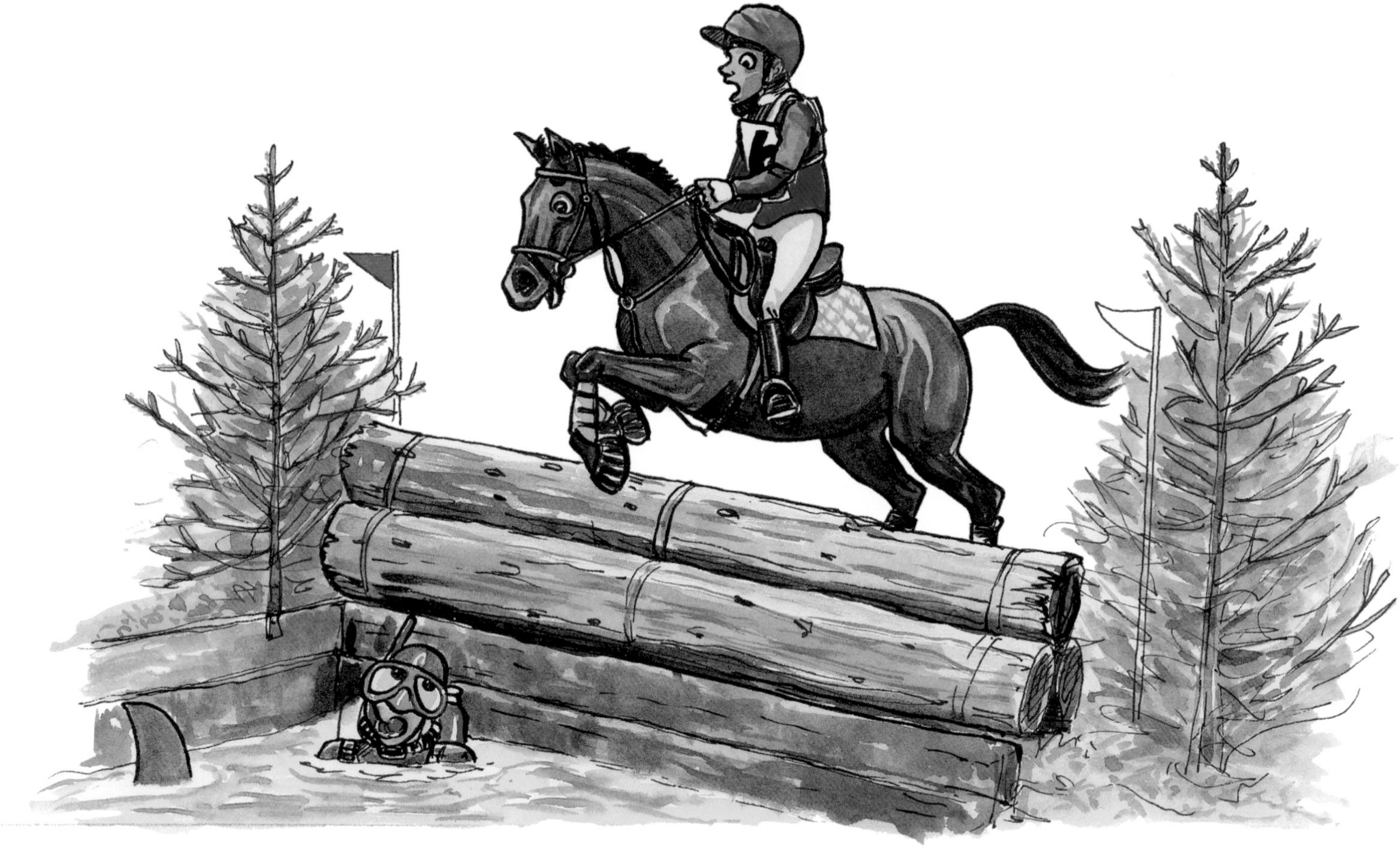

Natural Hazards

PONY CLUB...
...some types

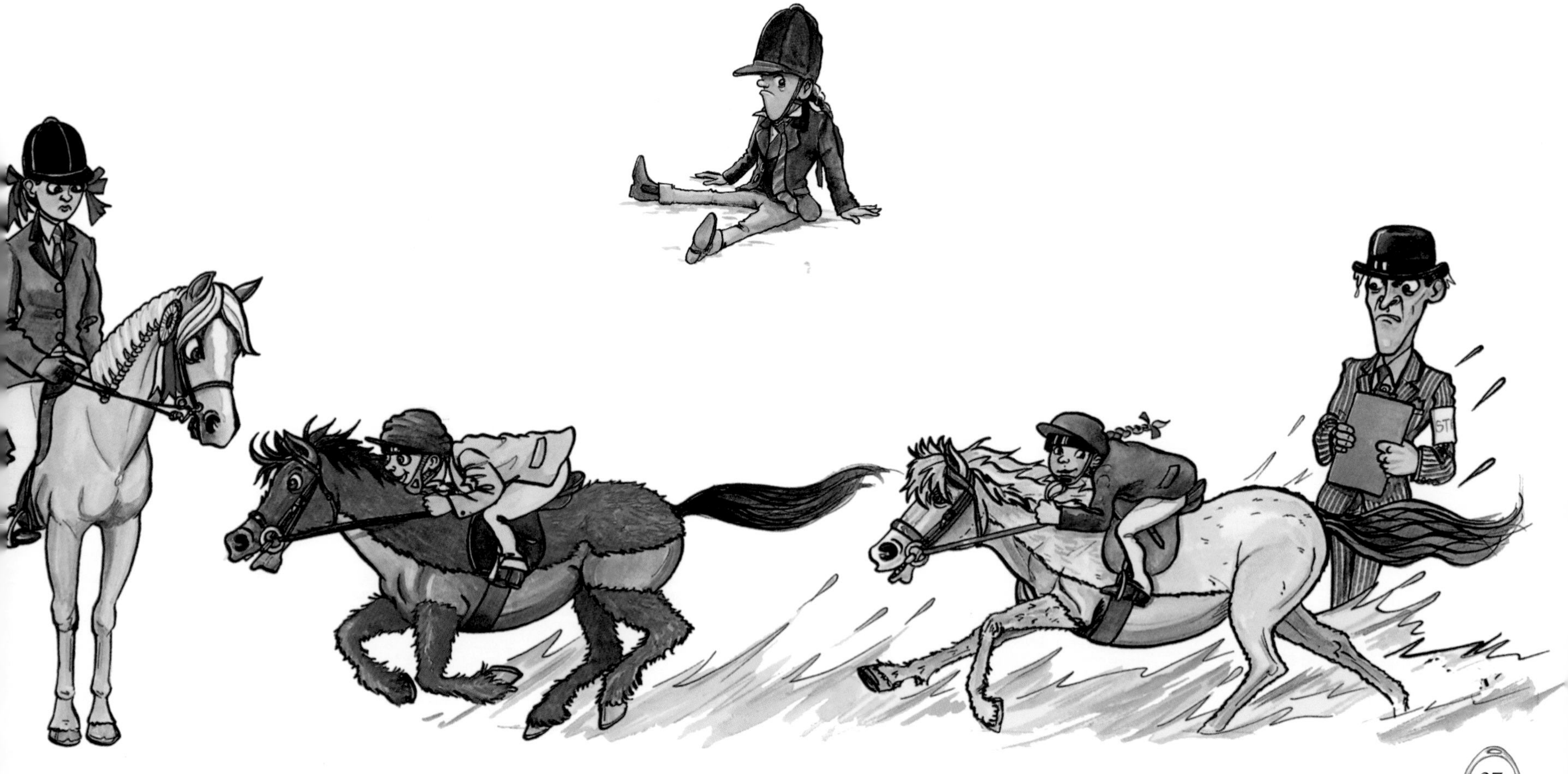

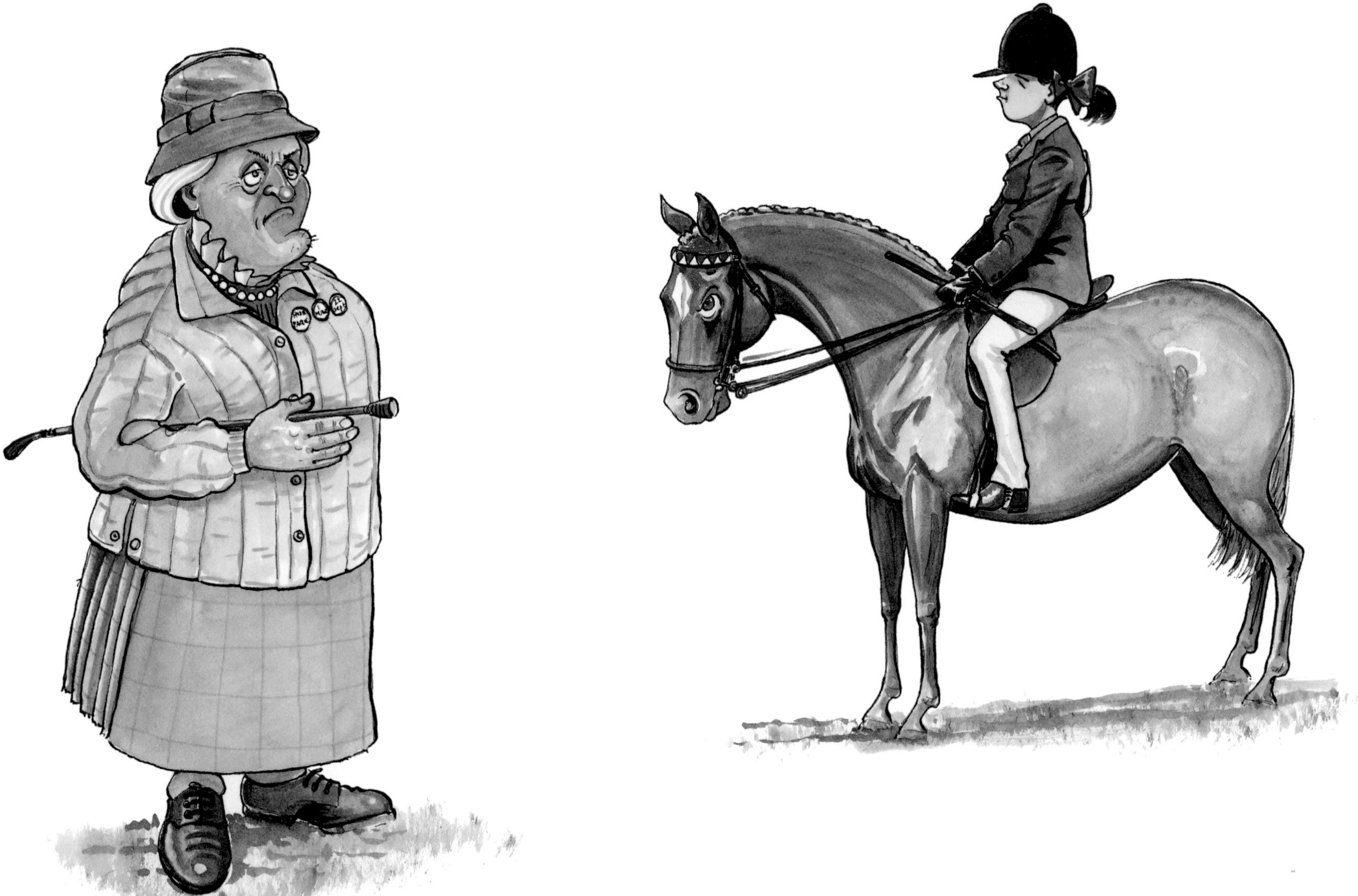

THE DISTRICT COMMISSIONER

The DC is not a figure to be taken lightly. Her position is clear, her opinion is forthright and her word is law. She is also and furthermore the final arbiter of taste and judgement and her decision is final. Decisions are there to be made and if anyone is going to make them it will be her. She chooses the teams and allocates the rides, calling her determinations to her adjutant who stands alert at her side with the clipboard and an eager expression and who'd like to be DC herself, of course, though the DC rather doubts if she's up to it. The DC splits up friends and mixes boys and girls willy-nilly. Political correctness is not on her agenda and she doesn't care who knows it. If they don't like it they can lump it. She doesn't like groups, won't have cliques and abhors gangs. Children should develop as individuals and learn how to muck in, get on and play for the team. Anything else is just woolly-headed thinking and leftist bleeding heart shilly-shallying and she's not having any of it. If a child isn't to be allowed to fall off from time to time dust itself down and jolly well get back on again without a whole raft of enquiries and paper work you might as well consign the whole generation to a gang of cotton wool wielding social workers and send them to hell in a handcart. Anyway, what else are collarbones for?

Parents, on the other hand, are dealt with much more vigorously. Letters are sent out well in advance listing their duties and obligations and their child's requirements for the purpose. Lists of jobs at the gymkhana, at the events, at camp. Responsibilities and rotas. She picks the teams for these too and if she deplores gaggling – as she calls it – among the children, she takes a positive delight in creating the most unlikely pairings among the grown-ups. It's good for them, she reckons. How are children to learn how to rub along with each other if their parents can't make the effort once in a while?

Lists of clothes, lists of tack, lists of kit. These are necessities and they should be functional and clean and fit for the purpose. If you haven't got them then they must be bought, begged, borrowed or otherwise procured. The DC cannot bring herself to say stolen; even in jest. There are regular sales of second hand gear – tack, clothing, harness, rugs, tools, saddlery, you name it – organised within the branch, organised by her, where such stuff can be collected if it can't be bought new. There's nothing wrong with second hand, after all, even if these days some people would rather go without than be seen in hand-me-downs and cast-offs. Twaddle! The DC was brought up on cast-offs and hand-me-downs and is not above the occasional rummage through a junk shop or a car boot sale even now. After all, something that has survived thus far probably has a bit of life in it yet. More, in the DC's view, than the modern equivalent, if the truth be known because it was made to last while the modern stuff is feeble my comparison and comes apart at the seams after no work flat.

In her vintage Volvo, the DC, from her lion's mane coiffure and WRNS sweater, through her early Puffa and sensible tweed skirt, to her sturdy shepherd's crook and harness leather saddlebag satchel is a walking testament to her own opinions that if it is made properly in the first place it will give decent service and last forever with a bare minimum of care and attention.

And the scariest part about it is that it all actually works. Stuff does happen on time, children do develop, successes are achieved and prizes are won.

The fact that the DC was once a young mum standing petrified with her teenage daughter while the then DC tore strips off the pair of them in front of everybody there assembled for the sloppiness of their turnout, the poverty of their performance and the fact that they were late into the bargain is a secret vouchsafed only to a very few. Such as the fragile single mum who stands on the fringes of the proceedings who is new to the area and to the branch and who has scrimped and saved to get her child to camp in good order and is cold-shouldered and cut by the more prosperous and established parents but who offers to help and contributes what she can and who will make a useful committee member in due season and who might very well end up as DC herself one day, if the DC is any judge of character. Which she is. If, that is, the current DC ever retires. Or dies. Neither of which seems likely.

29

THE CAMP COMMANDANT

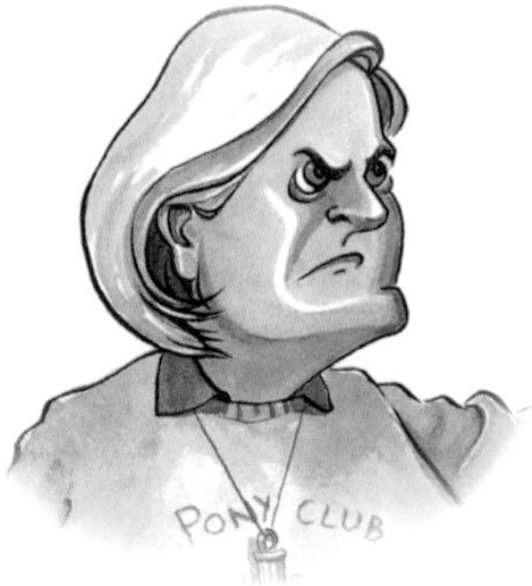
PONY CLUB

They call her Matilda the Hun. Which is odd since she's not German and she isn't called Matilda; but then children's minds work in strange ways. And in the view of the children – and not a few of the grown-ups for that matter – Strangeways is where Matilda the Hun would be most comfortable and where she may very well end up. And anyway, she answers to Matilda. No one knows why. Always has.

She rouses the camp at first light – or very shortly thereafter, though it seems like first light for those who really only went to sleep what seems to be a few minutes ago and that includes most of the happy campers and not a few of the not so happy grown-ups – by blowing reveille on her hunting horn which is the sort of thing that Matilda the Hun can do. And she follows this up with a stream of orders through the megaphone which lives on a strap round her wrist and which is closer still to her heart. 'Rise and shine you horrible lot! Feed and water ponies and then showers all round and down to the cookhouse for breakfast! Parents – first shift on breakfast duty in five minutes! Please! Let's be having you, people! Chop-Chop-Work-Work-Busy-Busy-Bang-Bang!'

Matilda the Hun also has a whistle which sees a good deal of action throughout the day. 'On my whistle we'll change the rein!' 'On my whistle dismount, into the sack, round the cone, back into the saddle!' 'On my whistle you nice chaps will change the course for the jump off!' 'All ready? On my whistle then!'

It is rumoured that there was once a Mr Hun. There are rumours that there still is and that he is variously locked up somewhere at the stables where Matilda holds sway and runs courses for problem horses and difficult children or that he did a runner in the dim and distant not long after he woke up from whatever dream he inadvertently married Matilda in.

The truth is, inevitably, more pedestrian though it goes some way to explaining Matilda. There was indeed a Mr Hun – or perhaps Herr Hun – and he was, if anything, more Hunnish even than Matilda. He came straight out of the Guards and took the view that everything in life benefited from having clearly defined boundaries which he duly applied to friends, relations, horses, dogs and Matilda without regard for age, sex, rank or station. One thing which did not respond well to boundaries was his elderly MGB sports car which duly went into a flyover on the way back from a regimental reunion leaving Matilda with little or nothing but a string of aging hunters and some firm ideas on how best to train the next generation of more or less anything.

Accordingly she immersed herself in the Pony Club and has been running summer camps now for more years than anybody cares to remember or dares to mention.

'OK, you lot, clean teeth, rub down, tack up, buff and puff and form up in teams in the main ring in fifteen minutes! Instructors' and assistants' briefing now please! On my whistle!'

On the other hand, of course, it must be admitted that camp always runs smoothly and when the team – which Matilda selects and trains, of course – turns out to compete they look the business and go like the proverbial clappers and are rarely off the top of whatever podium is going. So no one is going to rock the boat or launch a coup in the direction of Matilda the Hun. Which is fine by them and fine by Matilda. And certainly no one is going to call her Mrs Penfeather. Let alone Florence.

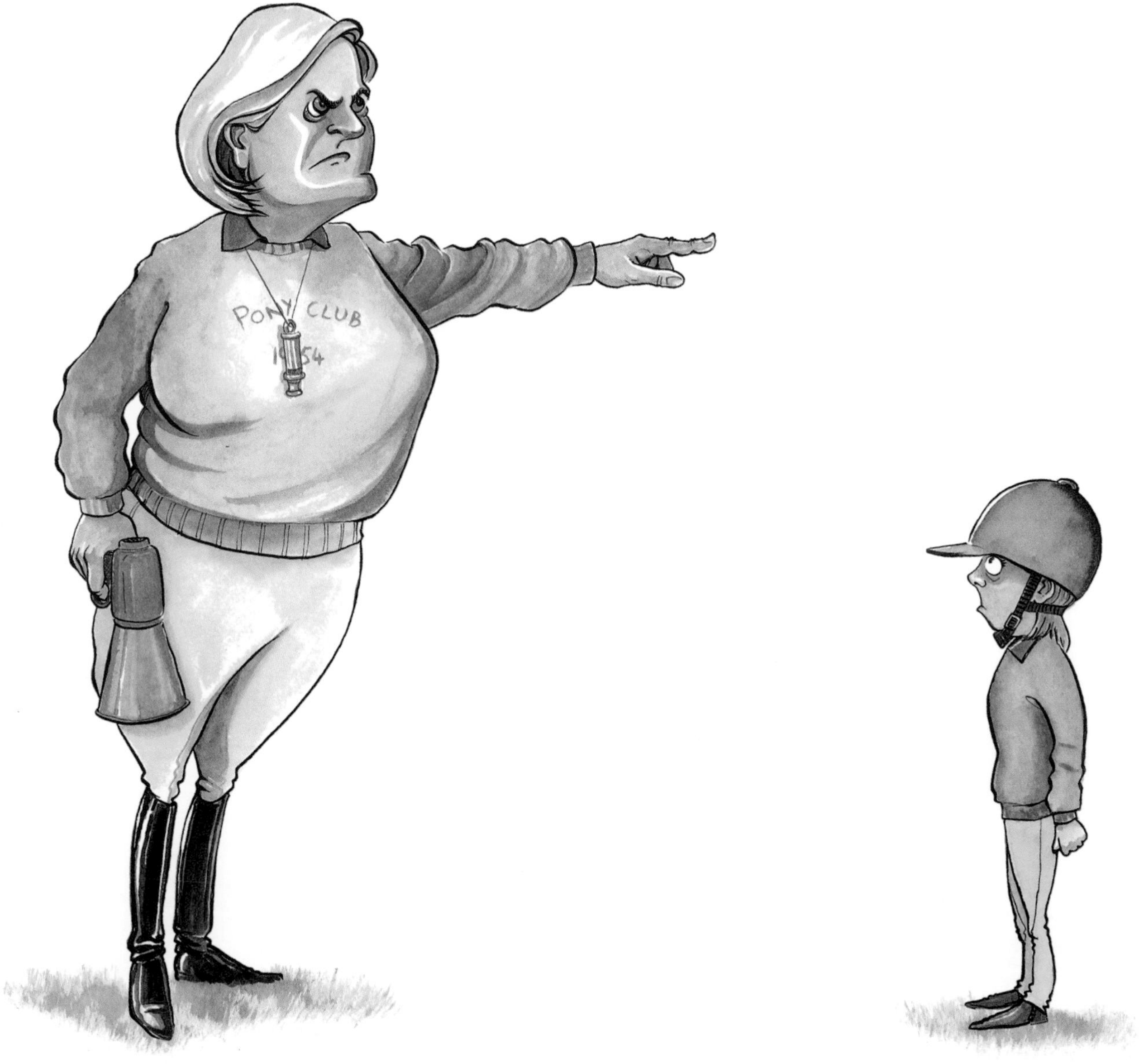
PONY CLUB
1954

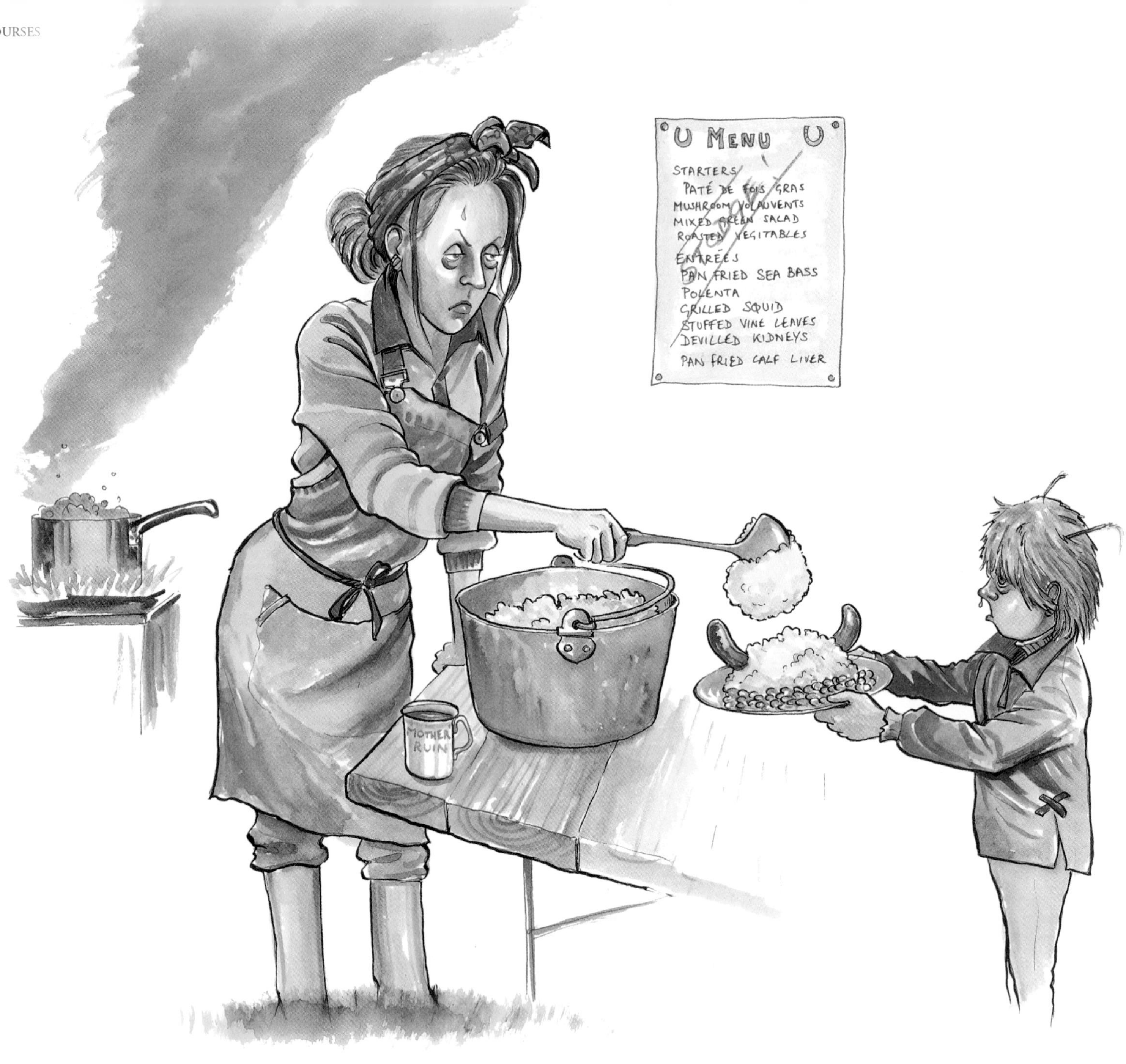
MENU
STARTERS
PATÉ DE FOIS GRAS
MUSHROOM VOLAUVENTS
MIXED GREEN SALAD
ROASTED VEGITABLES
ENTRÉES
PAN FRIED SEA BASS
POLENTA
GRILLED SQUID
STUFFED VINE LEAVES
DEVILLED KIDNEYS
PAN FRIED CALF LIVER
MOTHER RUIN

COOKING FOR CAMPERS

'Ring the damn bell and let the little brutes at the trough then!'

Pile it high and keep it simple. Don't dress the salad. Don't make a salad. Don't even mention a salad. Poor Annabel. She started the week with such high hopes. She was just so conscious of, well, not really pulling her weight where the Pony Club was concerned. It wasn't that she didn't want to; it's just that – to be honest – horses are not really her thing quite, being, as they are, slightly like some of the other Mums, if the truth be known, rather large and solid and ever so slightly scary. And large and solid and scary is not Annabel at all. Annabel is a bit of a poodle actually whereas some of the others are more mastiff than not as, a matter of fact.

So when the DC asked for volunteers to man – or woman – the camp kitchen, Annabel's hand went up like a shot. Here was something she could do. Leith's cordon bleu may be more years ago than Annabel cares to remember and her season in Verbier little more than a soft focus memory but a quiche is a quiche for all that and Annabel can fold a napkin nine ways till Tuesday. It was full of high hopes and girlish expectation that Annabel pulled her little Fiesta up behind the kitchen block filled to brimming with wooden spoons, soufflé dishes and more ramekins than you could shake a Magimix at. The trouble is: this is camp. And camp

doesn't do ramekins. And campers don't do salads. Some at least may be teenage girls for the rest of the year and may indeed be concerned with hipsters and the proper application of eyeliner and whether or not beige is this year's black and toying with a tuna nicoise but for this week they are pony-copers first, last and in between and that means regular, large scale injections of protein and carbohydrate in more or less equal quantities and it doesn't matter a damn what it looks like as long as it fills the void and does the job.

Annabel swore blind that she would not allow her menus – which she has been pondering and designing for weeks in advance so as to achieve just the right balance between energy and aesthetics – to be reduced to just so much institutional fodder. But camp is an institution after all and institutions run best on institutional food. That means bacon and eggs for breakfast; doorstop sarnies for lunch and pizza and chips for supper. Or maybe snaggers and mash. Or burger and chips. Anything probably as long as

it has chips with it. And a gallon of tomato sauce with everything. It may not be modern. It sure isn't nouvelle; but it's easy to recognise; manageable when you are on the brink of exhaustion after ten hours in and around the saddle following a minging night which included a raid on the boys' tents, a water fight with the juniors and a seriously ill-advised showy-offy overindulgence with an indifferent Chilean merlot. And it works.

Annabel started the week in a smart white apron and mob-cap and restored herself between shifts by sipping herbal tea. She missed her Poggenpohl double oven terribly and was horrified to find that the ghastly industrial complex that she was supposed to be cooking in contained no steamer for the children's vegetables. She wrote out her daily menus on a blackboard and stressed the healthy options and vegan alternatives.

Who is this now who stands behind the counter, ladle in hand and with a knotted handkerchief bandana about her brow. There is a mug nearby from which she slugs from time to time but it is quite another herbal remedy it contains today. Mostly gin. Her fleece and jeans and indeed her wellies are splashed and stained. Can this indeed be she?

'Ring the damn bell and let the little brutes at the trough then!' says Annabel and takes another gulp from her mug.

The Campers

Claudia is tired and sore and homesick and missing her Boo-Rabbit. She has never been separated from Boo-Rabbit for so long and she wants his comforting snuggle like she wants her next breath. Claudia cried herself to sleep for the first three nights of camp but now there are no tears left and no Boo-Rabbit either. Her sleeping bag is all itchy into the bargain, probably because Claudia has most of her clothes on because she doesn't like the others seeing her My Little Pony jim-jams and has scarcely done more than dab her face with a flannel each evening because she won't use the showers which are communal and unpredictable and anyway she has trouble reaching the taps.

She is as the consequence acutely conscious that she is beginning to pong which will just give her so-called team-mates another excuse to be perfectly horrid to her on top of all the other reasons they have found already. She hates them. She hates them all. She hates camp. She loathes baked beans and she misses her Boo-Rabbit. She even hates Dandy because he trod on her foot today and all they did was laugh and when she cried because it really, really hurt they all just kept laughing and now she's got a huge bruise on her foot anyway and all they did was call her Claudia Clodhopper which made her want to cry again even if she didn't. It wasn't her fault she dropped the flag in the relay and she wouldn't be the last on muster every morning if the others would just stop hiding her girth

or moving the bucket she stands on to put Dandy's bridle on. It's not fair and she hates them all and she wishes she was at home with her Boo-Rabbit. And to make matters worse, as if matters could get any worse, she can hear them all giggling in the tent next door where they have decamped for a midnight feast with the Blues and where they are doubtless talking about her and calling her names and planning more horrid jobs for her to do and foul tricks to play on her and more names to call her and it is all so unfair and not even a Boo-Rabbit to make it even slightly better. And it's all awful and she hates it. So there.

Clive, strangely enough, would probably sympathise with Claudia. It was only a few years ago when Clive was a tick on his first camp and cried himself to sleep too. He had smuggled his Huggy-monster into his kitbag and woke up the first morning to find that his tent-mates had hanged it from one of the guy-ropes whence it had to be retrieved in full daylight by Miss Whissett while the whole camp – or so it seemed to a furiously red-faced and watery-eyed Clive – stood

about and hooted. Not least at Clive's Bat-jams. That was then. Now Clive is a strapping six-footer who is widely known to drink pints and has his own quad-bike at home which is, like, really, really cool. He wears spurs and polo boots with zips up the back and his whacker stuck in the side. The girls think that Clive is just the business and Clive is fully aware of the fact although he is still profoundly uncertain as to quite what to do about it which is probably just as well for all concerned. One response, which Clive finds works quite well, is to ignore all the girls all of the time beyond accepting their breathy offers to tack up his pony for him which lets Clive scrounge an extra half hour in bed of a morning and for which he thanks them with no more than a grunt from behind the lank hank which flops across his face which the girls think is so dashing but which Clive knows is masking a fierce boil emerging on his forehead as the consequence of the thick end of a week living on fried breakfasts, chips with everything and Mars Bars. This is Clive's last camp. Ever. Until, that is, he joins the SAS or 2 Para. or the marines where Clive will devote every anti-interrogation technique ever taught to making sure that no one ever finds out he was in the Pony Club, let alone went to camp, because they'd probably do a deal more than nail his Huggy-monster to a tent post. Plus ça change.

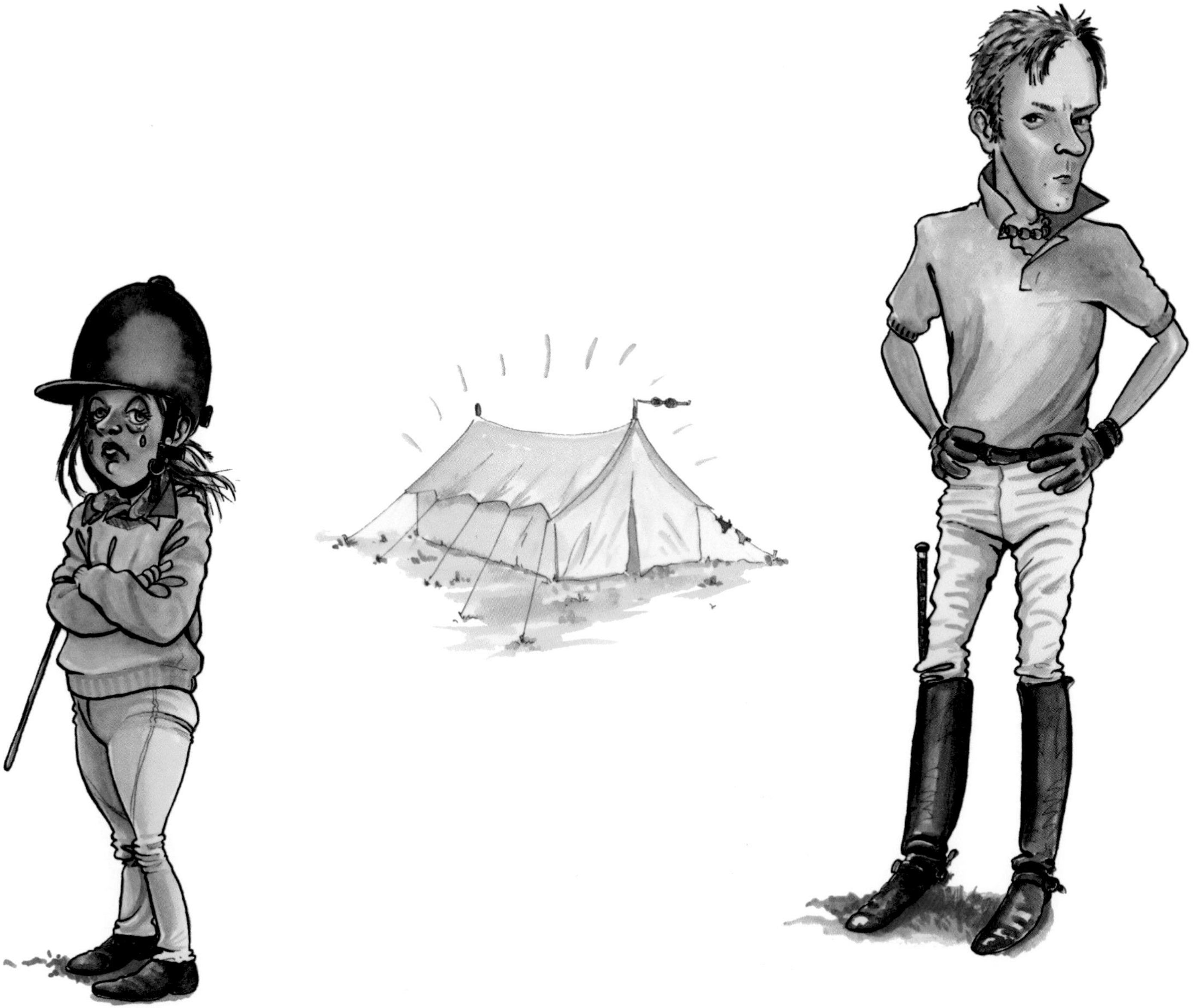

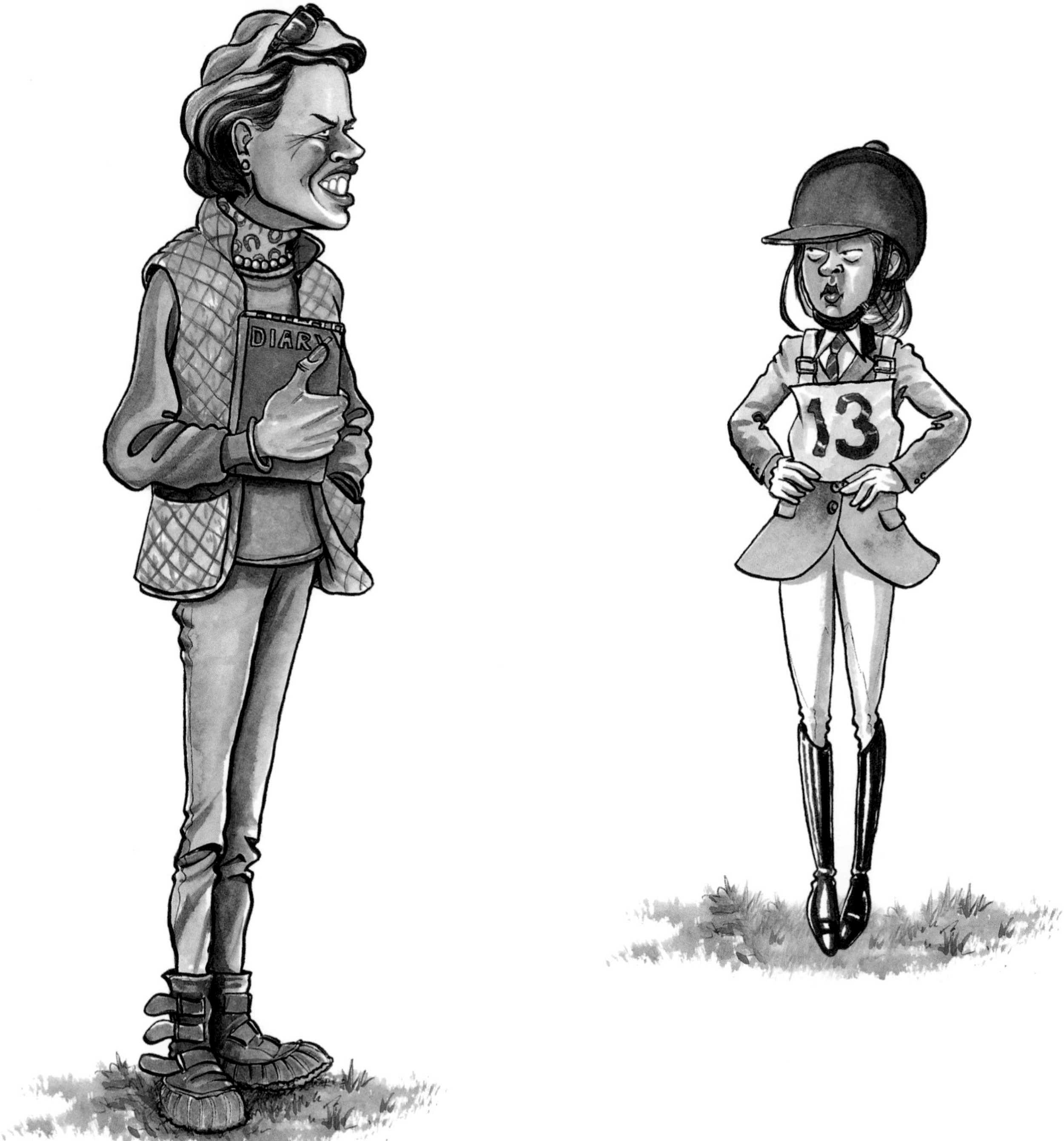
DIARY
13

Portia's Mum

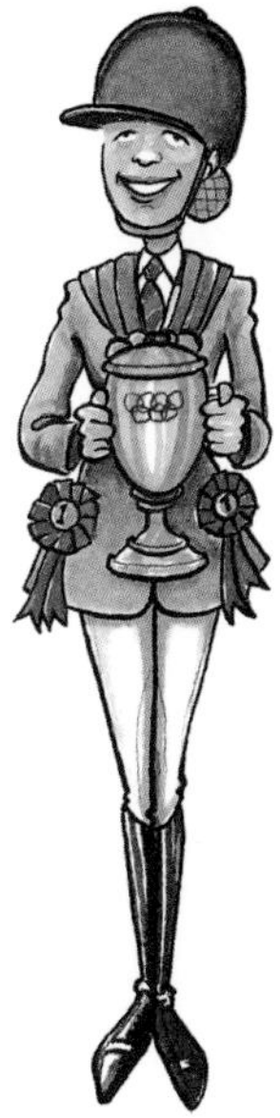

Portia is freckled, fifteen and well on the way to fulfilling her Mum's frustrated ambition to be something serious in the three-day event world. She has a cracking three-quarter bred Irish hunter which they picked up for a song in a sale at Newmarket because it was a known problem horse and which has come on in leaps and bounds. Leaps and bounds being largely what it did for a goodly few months while Portia nursed sundry bruises and bites and a glorious black eye at one point, that Portia's Mum described as an honourable rite of passage, but which rather took the edge off Portia's debut at the Pony Club dance. Until Portia's Mum – who fancies herself as a bit of a horse whisperer on the quiet – took the brute in hand while Portia was away at school and taught it the rules of the road and, for that matter, tracks, and cross country and show jumping and dressage into the bargain. Now it performs admirably and everyone says that Portia has every chance of taking him all the way, if she wants to. Not that anybody asks her. Least of all her Mum.

So all the early mornings of mucking out and all the evenings of schooling in the paddock behind the house and all the lost weekends thrashing the Rice wooden trailer up and down the country behind the old LWB Defender, because Daddy wouldn't spring for a Disco and Portia's Mum refuses point blank to be seen in his Range Rover which she thinks is just too plutocratic for words even if it is more comfortable and easier by miles, have started to pay off and Portia's in with a shout.

And Portia's tack may be secondhand and Portia may have to do all her plaiting and combing herself because Portia's Mum says that when she was Portia's age they couldn't afford new tack and anyway you get far more satisfaction from a good turnout if you've done it yourself and hard work never killed anyone and dressage judges will always be more generous to the struggling amateur with just her Mum in tow than to a rider with a six berth Mercedes lorry and a slack handful of scurrying grooms even if Daddy could afford it what with the stock market and redundancy looming and the house not even really finished and when I was your age I had to do everything for myself and it didn't do me any harm, now did it? A point on which Portia is strategically and sensibly mute.

And when Portia is showing signs of flagging in her relentless pursuit of the rosette strewn path to Badminton, Burghley and beyond Portia's Mum is always ready to raise the spectre of her selfless sacrifice over the years of gymkhanas and camps and one day events and two-day events and scrimping and saving just so that Portia never went without ponies and Portia's ponies never went without and where would Portia be today if it weren't for the continuing support of Portia's Mum weekend in, weekend out Portia's Mum would like to know?

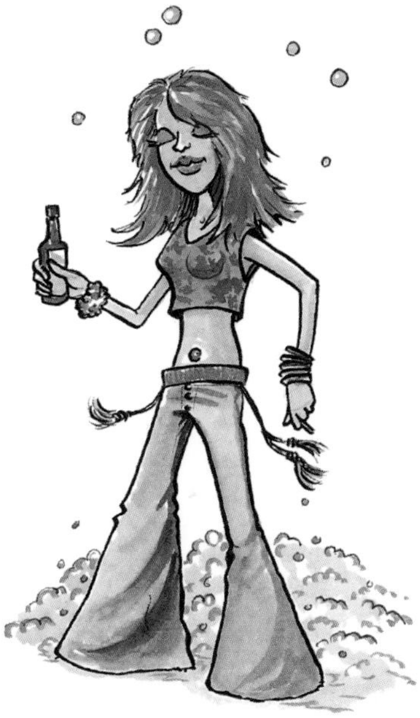

And Portia's Mum dreams of Tidworth and Gatcombe and Hickstead and sponsorship and Great Britain trials and who knows what beyond that; though the smile that beams from behind the trophies in her dreams may be closer to her own than to Portia's if the truth be known. And Portia dreams of boy bands and glittery nail polish and jeans so wide you could lose a small army in them. Not that anybody asks her what she dreams of. Least of all her Mum.

CHERYL

Cheryl doesn't really like horse riding. Truth be told she doesn't really like horses. God's honest? They scare her witless. Even the little ones. The wotsits. Ponies. Shetlands! Shetland ponies. No higher than the rhinestone buckle on her chamois pedal-pushers but with a mean glint, know what she means? And as for them big buggers, hunters and that, well she won't go near them. Not for all the tea. They asked her to hold onto one down at the horse riding stables while someone gave someone a leg-over – leg-up? whatever – and it pulled and Cheryl squeaked and it pulled again and Cheryl squeaked some more and then let go and someone said 'Grab his head for Chrissakes, woman!' but she couldn't possibly what with it snorting right in her face and everything; so she stood there in her Nicole Farhi faux leopardskin kitten heel slingbacks with her hands over her eyes and people were shouting at her and there was stamping and snorting and swearing and all sorts and when she opened her eyes there was chaos and everyone looking at Cheryl like it was her fault.

So now Cheryl attends weekly at another horse riding establishment altogether on the other side of town where her reputation has yet to permeate and

where they don't mind that she calls it horse riding and that little Kerry-Jo – for whose social advancement and personal edification the whole farrago has been undertaken – has no talent, less inclination to learn and no interest in it flat to boot. She puts up with it because Mummy says she has to and Kerry-Jo knows that if Mummy says you have to, you have to, because you're too young to run away from home anyway and wise enough beyond your years to see that putting up with it wins prizes in the form of loads of new clothes and trainers and CDs and a DVD in your bedroom and loads of cool stuff for all of which an hour a week, albeit on a Saturday, plodding round a sand school on a pony on a leading rein is not too great a price to pay when all is said and done.

And the stables put up with it because frankly plodding round a sand school with a fat kid on a pony on the lunge for an hour a week at the rates they charge Cheryl is the easiest money going and until she finds out the extent to which they are overcharging her – or

perhaps until she cares – they are quite happy to make her and the fat kid welcome and ensure that the oldest and slowest pony is tacked and ready at the appointed hour and not involve Cheryl further in proceedings. And that suits Cheryl just fine because she doesn't like horses but she knows that if she and Daryl and Kerry-Jo are going to make a success of this back-to-nature, countryside, upper crust sort of a lifestyle then someone in the family has to ride, preferably to hounds and with royalty for choice but a start has to be made somewhere and this is as good as any as far as she can see. Anyway the alternative is shooting and if Cheryl is frightened by horses then she is terrified of guns and the very idea of watching something actually shot just turns her stomach. So riding it is and if Kerry-Jo doesn't like hunting then she can play polo instead and meet princes that way. And loads of celebrities too. Actually polo is better than hunting because you get princes and celebrities. And supermodels. Even Daryl will like polo. Yes. Polo, it is. She'll tell the horse riding stables next week when Kerry-Jo has her lesson and then she will set about buying what's necessary. She'll need a new 4x4 for sure. Do BMW do one in sky-blue?

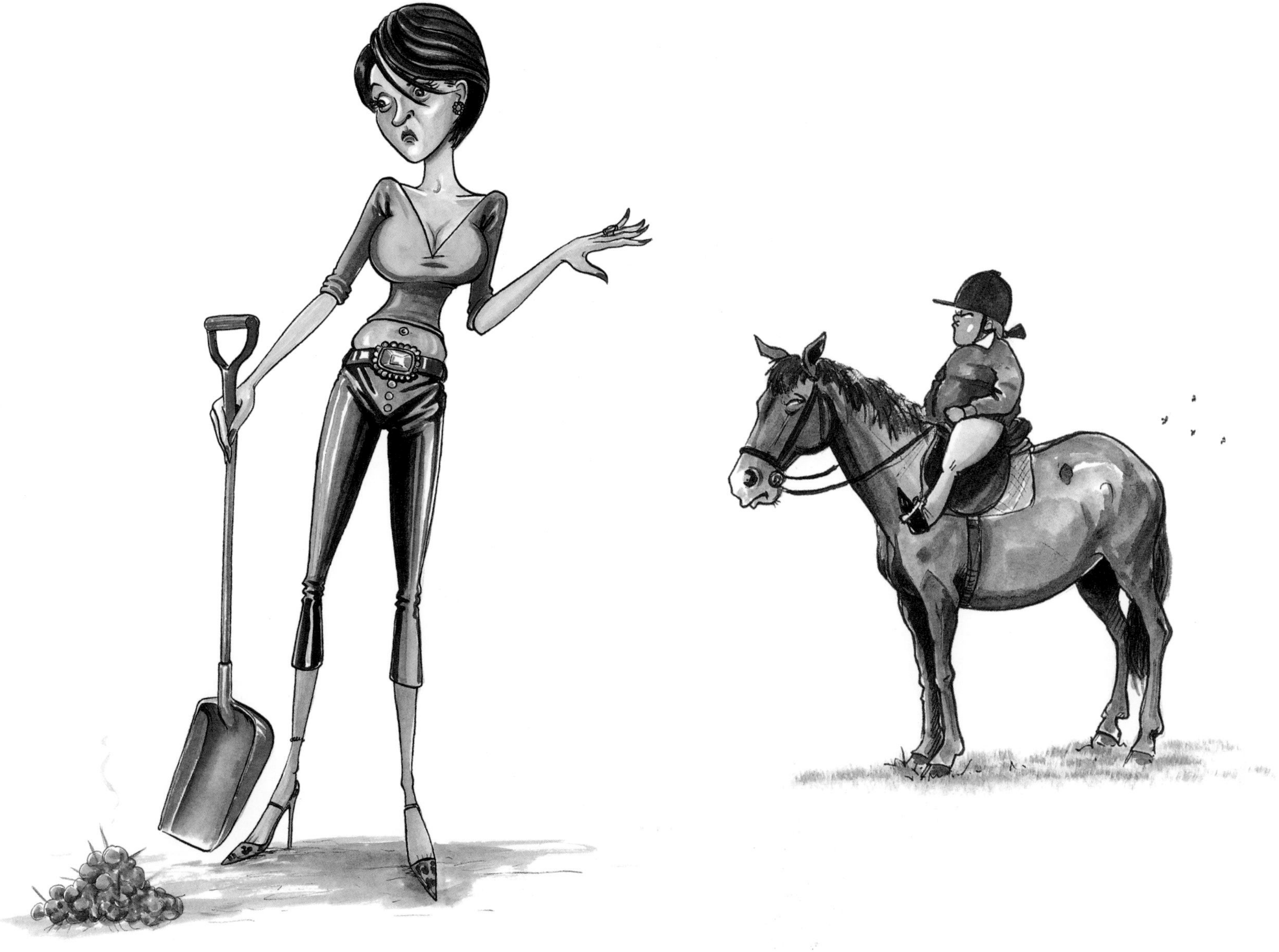

THE SHOW OFF

Veronica is by *House & Garden* out of *Interiors* and the show ring is just an extension of the garden room linen effect in three easy steps or a handcrafted farmhouse kitchen with minimalist features incorporating Welsh slate finishes. Veronica has downloaded every show class in the country onto her Blackberry and has been cross referencing them with her seasonal colourings and fabrics databases in order to establish just exactly what she will have to wear on any given day to have the maximum impact on the judges short of poking them in the eye with a sharp stick.

The schedules and the colour schemes are then faxed through to the stables in good time for them to ensure that the necessary browbands, saddles, reins, girths, ribbons and bandages can be washed, polished, waxed, rinsed, pressed and laundered in anticipation of her arrival in the country on Friday lunchtime. Then there are the judges to be considered before squaring either Jocasta's headmistress or Damian's housemaster to allow one unfortunate child or the other out early at the weekend to complete the ensemble. 'I know that it's not strictly in the curriculum' she warbles,

come Wednesday as one or other educationalist cavils at the suggestion of yet another lost weekend, 'but I do think the spirit of competition has such a rounding effect on the children and they do enjoy it so!' A strategic marriage, which was reported in all the quality monthlies, to a suitably tall, properly established – if somewhat older and crucially richer – husband, was quickly followed by a matching pair of appropriately photogenic children and an even more strategic separation. Divorce, after all, would have meant giving up either the town house or the place in the Cotswolds and might have jeopardised the cash-flow of Veronica's design consultancy, not to mention upsetting the children. By maintaining effective dialogue with her husband ('e-mail is such

a boon. Communication without conversation!') and establishing rigorous routines, Veronica is able to occupy both houses and oversee their continuous redecoration for his account and her satisfaction without the irritant of actually ever seeing him.

And at weekends she tears herself away from her work to support the children in the show ring. Showing suits Veronica. Eventing is too sweaty by half; show jumping wouldn't get her into the ring; dressage is just too dull. The show ring has it all.

The fact that Damian would rather keep goal for the Colts hockey and that Jocasta considers that the only sensible reason for having a pony is to hunt as hard and as fast as possible at every opportunity is dismissed with a wave of a well manicured hand.

For Veronica the look of the thing is all. The purpose of the pony is to populate the paddock that adjoins the house that contains the furniture that supports the vases which show the flowers that highlight the tones of the fabrics which make the curtains complement the rugs and reflect the purpose of the overall design which is to emphasise the exquisite taste and deft execution of the designer herself. To wit Veronica.

TEDDY

The children wanted a pony and their parents wanted the children to have a pony and a pony was duly acquired to the delight of all concerned. He was round and shaggy and cuddly and looked so like a woolly bear that he was inevitably christened Teddy. And for a season Teddy was the apple of the family's collective eye and was rigorously groomed on a daily basis. Indeed if the children could not be found elsewhere it was more likely than not that they would be in the newly fenced-off old orchard diligently applying the dandy brush or the hoof-pick while Teddy stood obligingly as the tinies crawled over him brushing and picking and combing and cosseting.

But school holidays do not last forever and early enthusiasms wane when the weather changes and the clocks go back and grooming is a cold and grimy business undertaken early in the mornings in the dark before the school day begins or in the chill of evening in the gloom when there is only the prospect of homework to follow and little chance to ride him anyway. And if Teddy is disinclined to play ball and trots off to the other end of the paddock and refuses to come to the headcollar like a good pony or issues the occasional nip to an injudiciously offered small bottom betimes which results in tears and recriminations and a bruise that lasts for a week or stands, inadvertently or otherwise, on a small foot, for example, where the agony is much magnified by being enclosed in a cold

and clammy welly then there is reason to suppose that Teddy's grooming is somewhat curtailed from time to time and perhaps understandably so.

Mum tries to remedy the situation at intervals but days are short and schedules cramped when there are three kids to deliver and collect from differing directions and a dizzying plethora of extracurricular activities to be managed. Rugby here, hockey there, remedial music and rehearsals for the school nativity, not to mention an apparently endless round of birthday parties. And Dad slumps in his chair of an evening and declares through gritted teeth that it wasn't his idea that they should have a damn pony and he's blowed if he's going to set off into the gloaming with a sugar lump and a curry comb to resolve his offspring's inability to measure up to their responsibilities.

So Teddy spends the autumn term whiling away the days in the paddock in the old orchard munching on the windfall apples and dreaming of the peat hags

back in Connemara until the Christmas hols arrive and with it the urgent need to go hunting.

By which time Teddy has grown unaccustomed to company and frisks away from children and parents alike and will not come to the collar even if offered sugarlumps and carrots by the bucketload and has developed a coat that would not disgrace a yak and which will defy any but an industrial clipper. A week of intensive grooming – shearing might be a better word – a visit from the farrier and several sackfuls of oats and high protein supplements later and Teddy looks the part. And at the meet he stands stoically still like a good pony should and chomps contentedly at the leading rein.

But when the hounds come tumbling out of their trailer and mill about among the field there assembled Teddy's back straightens and his tail twitches and a strange light comes into Teddy's eyes and Mum on the other end of the leading rein will have to have her wits about her today if she is not to be seen skiing across the plough behind a snorting destrier and a shrieking tot and giving the huntsman a run for his money.

But come January the festival is over, term time has come again and Teddy is back in the orchard whiling his days away between the trees, putting on weight under his old rug, growing his hair, thinking about hunting and dreaming of Connemara. Until Easter at any rate.

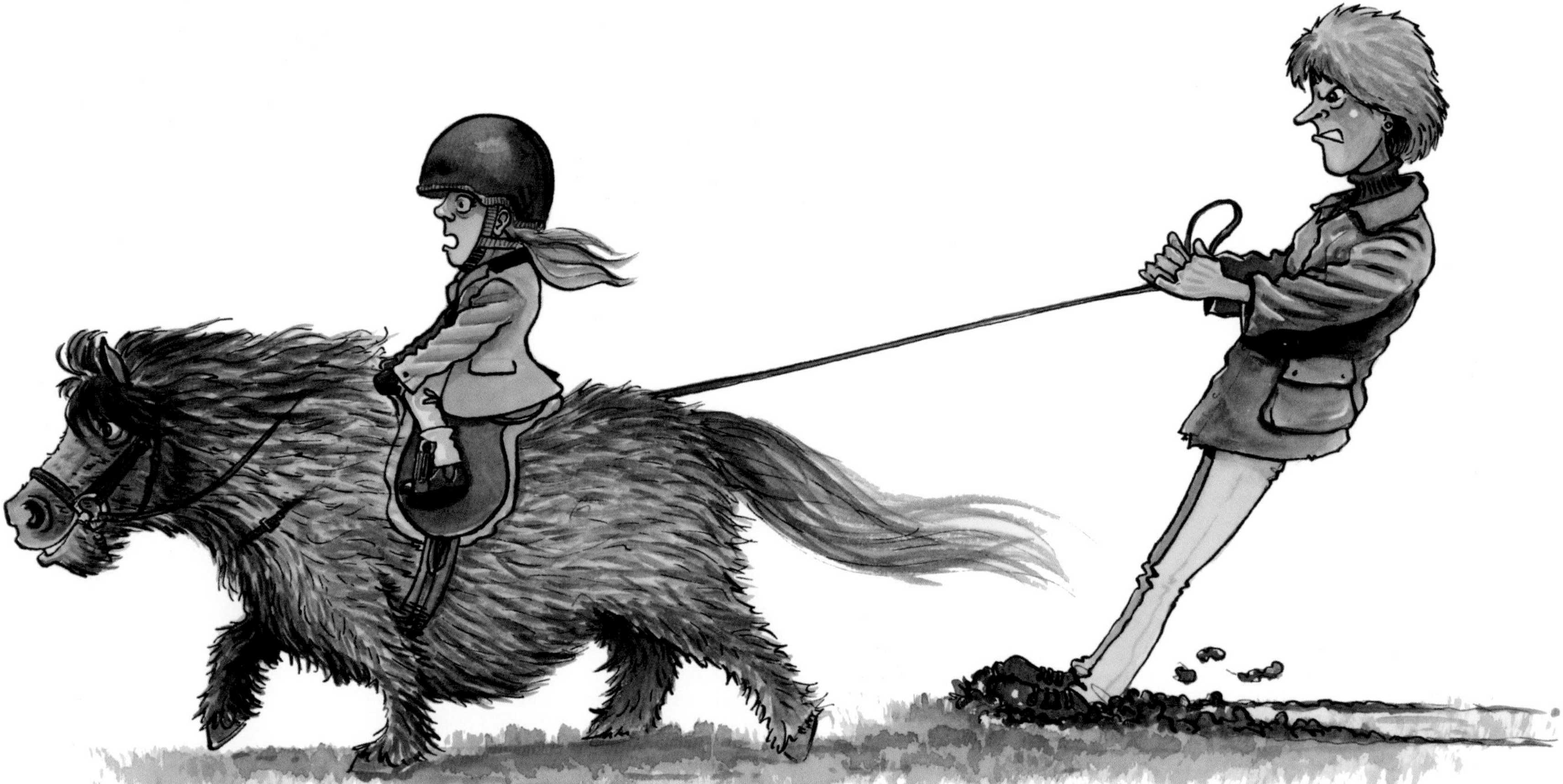

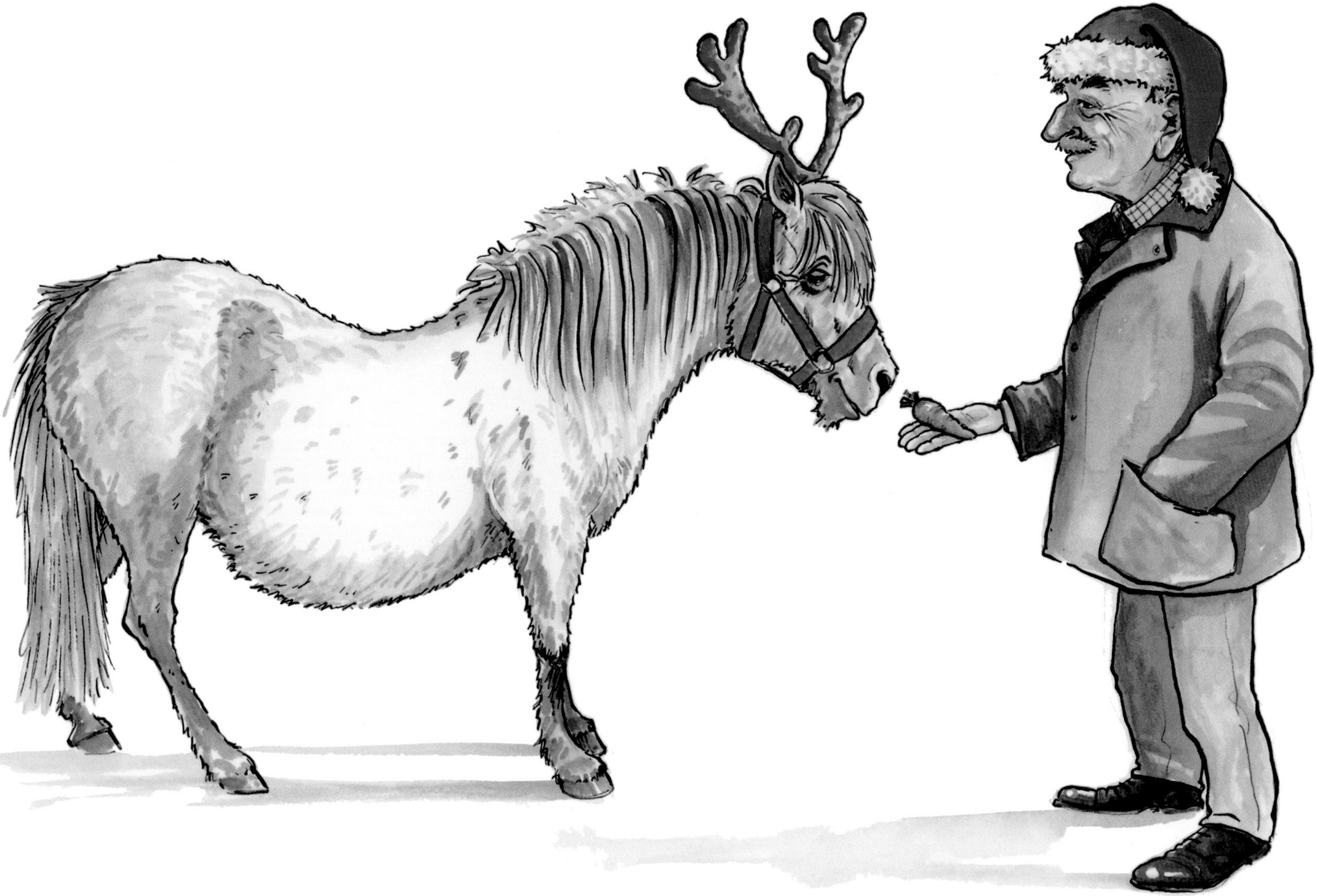

DANDY

Dandy is as old as the hills. Certainly nearer thirty than twenty though how old he is exactly is something of a mystery because he didn't really come with a passport after all because in those days ponies just didn't. He came from the New Forest although there again whether he was exported or simply swiped one day is a mystery shrouded in the mists of time. The chap who sold him to the Brigadier was not the sort of chap the Brigadier would have let on the place in the ordinary run of things being as he was the sort of rum cove that a chap didn't really do business with if a chap might be seen doing it, as it were. But the children wanted a pony and so the Brigadier had made enquiries locally and shortly thereafter this rum cove had arrived on the doorstep with the pony in a brokendown trailer behind a beaten up Land Rover and while the Brigadier was contemplating whether he should call someone or just pitch the bloke out on his ear the children had climbed into the trailer and adopted Dandy wholesale before he could come to a sensible decision. Accordingly modest sums changed hands and Dandy was installed in the looseboxes behind the big house and in due season was given the run of the paddocks beyond the ha-ha.

There he plodded backwards and forwards and round and round with one child or another in the saddle. From time to time he was persuaded to break into a trot and to address a row of cavallettis by one of the more adventurous children but when required to contemplate a striped pole balanced between a pair of half oil drums Dandy drew a line in the sand, dug his little hooves in and was not to be persuaded to become

fully airborne even for a second. At the gymkhana however Dandy shone. He could shimmy between the bending poles like a greased weasel and could judge the turns to a nicety to allow one pilot or another to drop the flag into the drainpipe in record time. He would stand patiently by while bean-bags were collected from buckets and then take off at a ferocious pace in a blur of dropped reins and flying stirrups, his little legs going like pistons in what became known over time as Dandy's tranter because it was much faster than a trot but despite the heels pummelling his ribs he could never be persuaded actually to change gear.

Even on his occasional outings to hounds Dandy could not be induced to move up a cog to a proper canter. Bright-eyed and bushy-tailed and definitely inspired by the occasion and the thrill of the chase Dandy's tranter would increase to unfeasible levels as he kept pace with the field without ever over the years breaking stride.

His tiny riders became less tiny. Some moved on to bigger mounts while others simply moved on. The Brigadier though never had the heart to get rid of him. Instead he was loaned to the local RDA where he continued to carry any number of excited tinies back and forth and round and round. Dandy was discussed again when the time came for the Brigadier himself to leave the big house to make way for a new generation who had more need of the space than he did, but it was only a short discussion – a formality, really – because while the grandchildren were only babies then, it was, as their mother stated firmly, only a matter of time before they were riding and who better to teach them than old Dandy, after all?

So now a whole new raft of Dandy wranglers are being carried back and forth and round and round the paddock beyond the ha-ha. His eyes may not be as good as they were but he can still trot through a row of cavallettis almost from memory and while the Dandy tranter may no longer sound like a drum roll over hard ground he can still make good time between the bending poles and he still stands patiently while small competitors thump into his broad flanks in an attempt at a flying remount having retrieved a fallen china egg.

And the Brigadier comes to see him in the paddock from time to time with a carrot or an apple and on Christmas morning there is still a stocking full of treats dangling from the loosebox door. And there will be for a few more years yet even though Dandy is as old as the hills. Or even older.

DANCING CORSAIR

In his racing days he was known as Dancing Corsair. Actually he was entered as Dancing Corsair. What he was known as round the yard was Fiery Fred on account of his ability to transform himself from the docile almost trancelike state, which seemed to be his natural and persistent mood, into a snorting, prancing firecracker in the blink of an eye and for no apparent or reliable reason. His trainer, his lad and his jockey all agreed that if only Fred could pull off this transformation at the start of a race and sustain the condition for the subsequent five minutes or so he would be so far ahead of the field that by the time the smoke cleared he'd be on the run in and home, free and laughing. And the trainer and the lad and the jockey agreed that they would be laughing into the bargain because there was no doubt that while Fred wasn't much to look at in the paddock with his drooping eyes and droppy pasterns they could pile on the stakes at long odds and if he ever came to life like that on the course they would be quids in.

Unfortunately though Fred was not in on the plan and while he continued to have his occasional fits of fire and fury – like in the yard and in the trailer and very occasionally even on the gallops – he signally failed ever to produce any kind of performance on

the course where he lolloped home half a dozen times several lengths behind the field despite the best efforts of the jockey to divert Fred's attention from the scenery to the issue in hand with his whip.

The crunch came when Fred had a spectacular moment in the yard after a morning ride out which resulted in the lad ending up with three cracked ribs and the trainer's Discovery with a large hoofprint in the driver's door. Fred was into the trailer and off to the next sale with his papers all in order and never a word said about violent mood swings.

Which is where Fiery Fred was spotted by Charlotte who knows just enough about horses to recognise that Fiery Fred should be just about perfect for her needs as a budding eventer but not enough about life to know that a horse sale is about the last place on earth that anyone, let alone a teenager – budding eventer or not – with a docile and chequebook-wielding father in tow, is ever going to find a bargain.

Which is how Fiery Fred – now called Charlie, for short – is now biding his time in the paddocks beside Charlotte's chequebook-wielding father's agreeable country house and guzzling up the Hi-Energy supplements with which Charlotte is feeding him to put a bit of sparkle back into his eyes and a bit of sheen on his coat and to make him into the Dancing Corsair that she knows she, and only she, can bring out of him.

And Fred knows that on a diet like this he could do a couple of laps of Aintree given half the chance, though it would take probably more than a Charlotte to keep him on course or indeed on the course, and is wondering whether he can hold his natural instincts in check for long enough to get another helping of nuts before letting off a bit of steam when Charlotte next takes him down to the ménage for a canter.

If you see a dozy-looking bay gelding, about 16 hands, leaning against the side of his stall at a sale somewhere near you any time soon with his eyes half closed and his feet crossed and you think that there's not a bad looking horse that might polish up nicely with a bit of care and attention and a snip at the price, say hello to Fiery Fred and give him a pat, if you like, and move swiftly on.

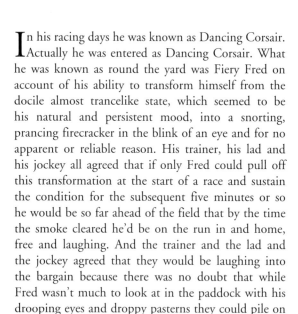

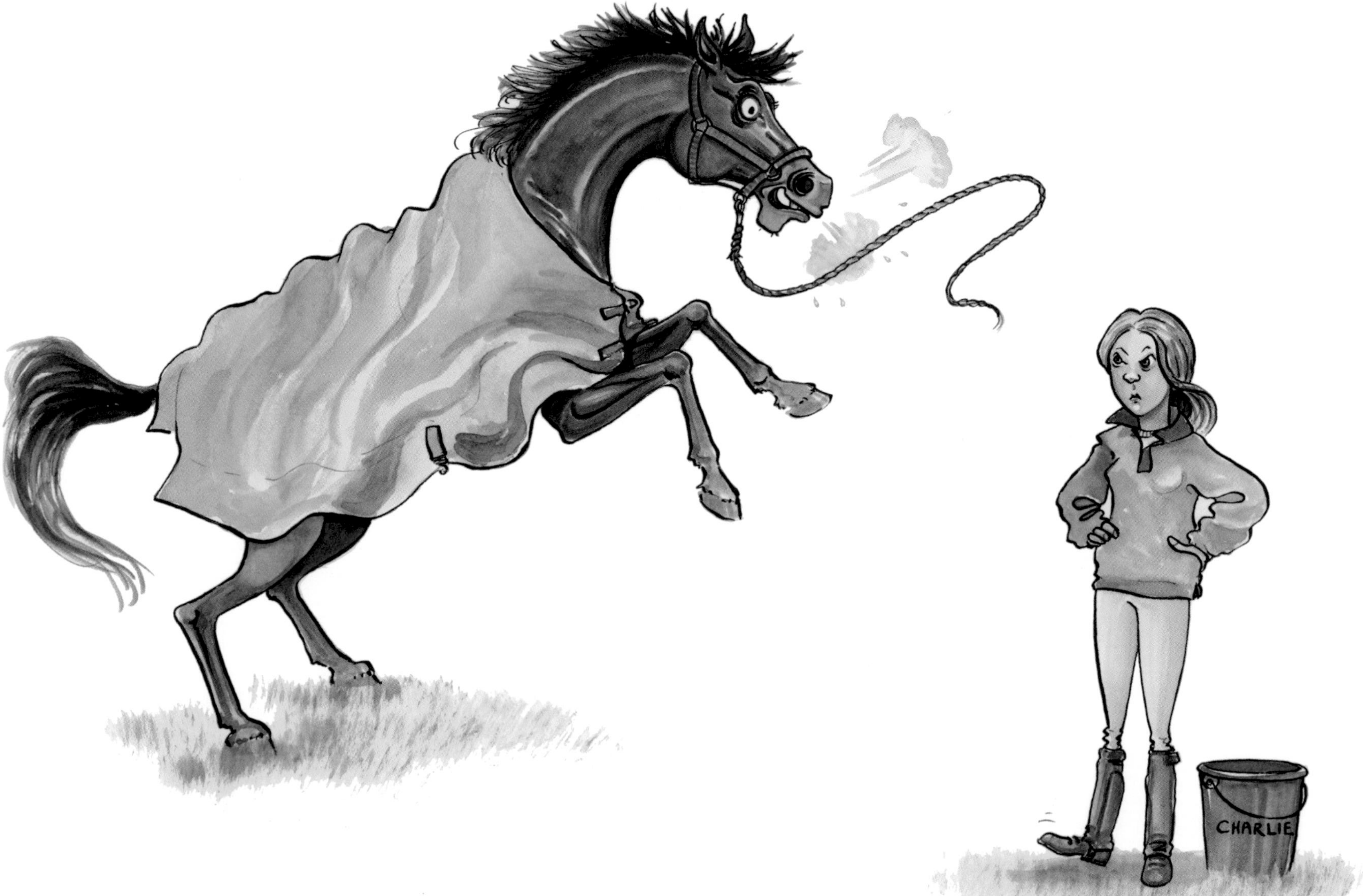
CHARLIE

DRESSAGE

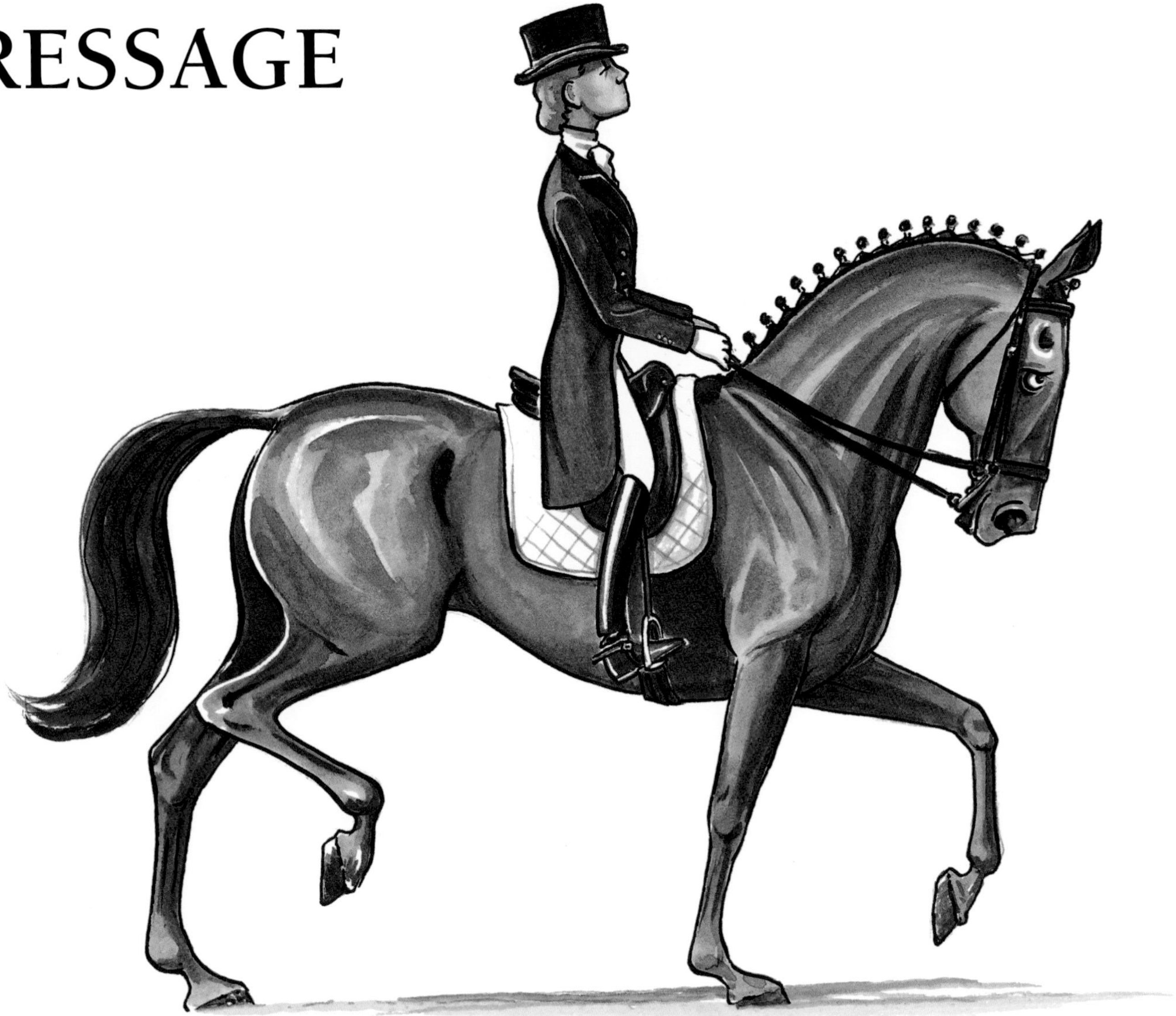

DRESSAGE...

...Diva

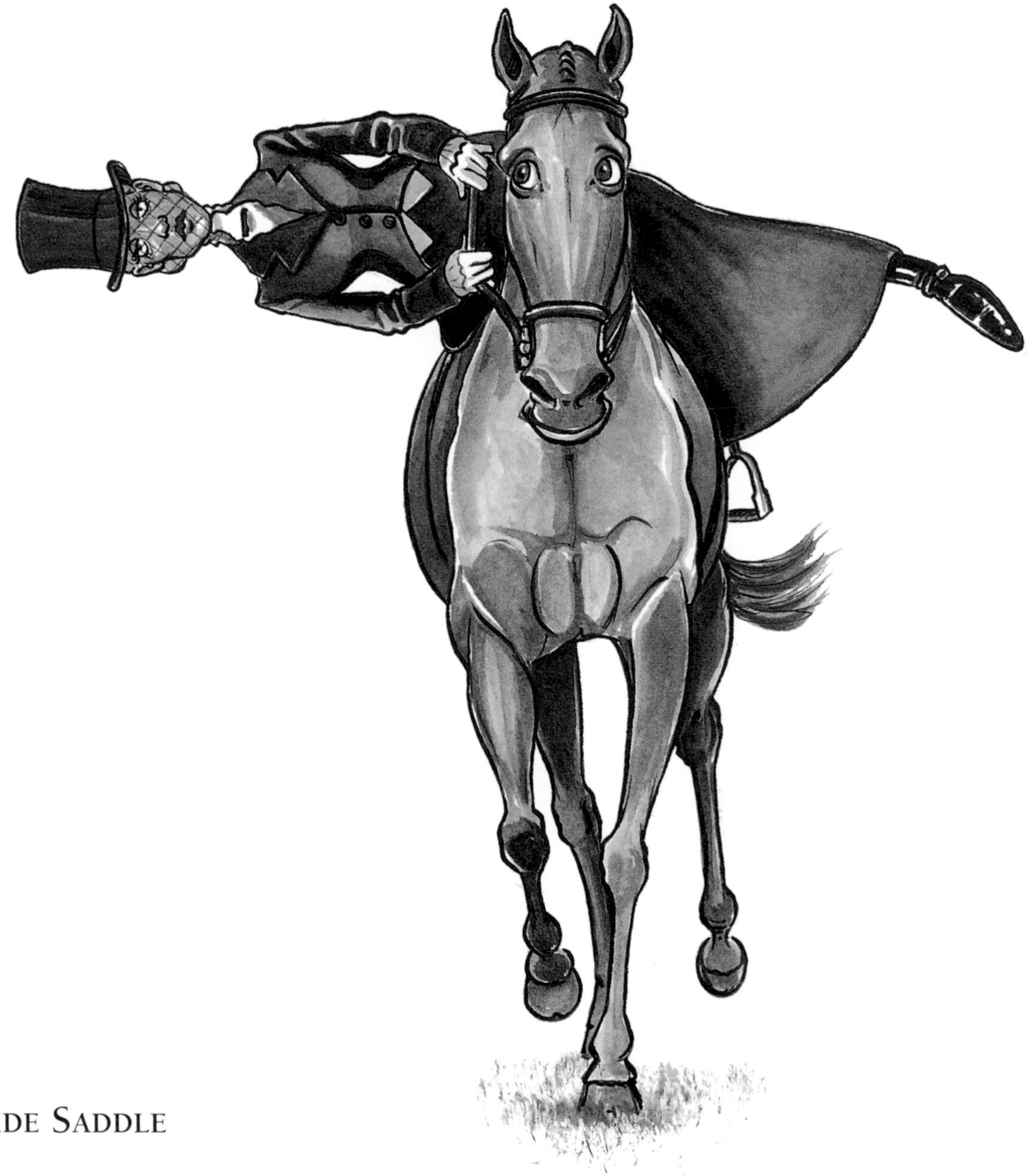

Side Saddle

TANGLE FOOT

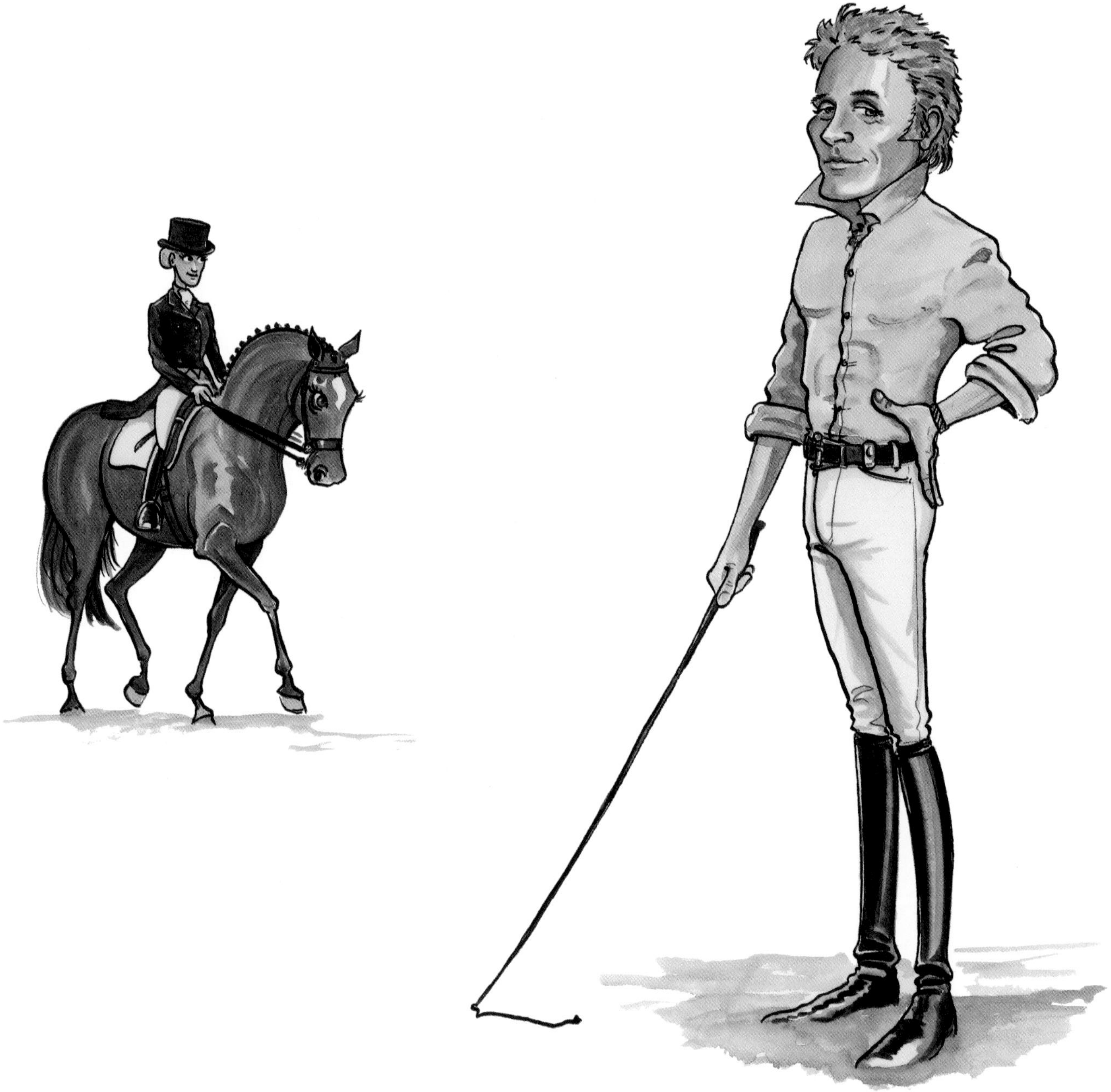

THE DRESSAGE INSTRUCTOR

Caspar is a vision in Harry Hall and White Stuff and Mountain Horse. All blond curls, freckles, Rayban and tan. Honest to god, the boy could stop traffic. It shouldn't be allowed. Most of his clients would have him about the place just for the look of the thing even if he didn't know his piaffe from his passage. They look forward to his visits each week as wilting flowers look forward to the sun. And when his hot little hatch zooms into the yard it is as if the day has got a little brighter. To be honest most of the ladies whom Caspar instructs aren't particularly interested in dressage. Indeed if they were interested in dressage then the sensible approach would be to buy a dressage horse and to practise for hours every day both in the saddle and on the rein, year round. That is how great dressage horses are made. But that would be to miss the point. Which is Caspar. Who comes, comes, comes to each of his ladies in turn to chivvy them round their own ménages with his dancing eyes and tumbling curls and canter banter. And they don't know whether

to mother him or butter him. What they do, though, is pay him. And while his fees are not extortionate by any means, and while he is worth every penny just for the little sunbeam that he is, let alone his undeniable expertise at travers and renvers, what they absolutely have to do is to show him off to their friends. Which means that the weekly session with Caspar – darling, if only it were! – becomes a ménage avec trios, or perhaps quartre, of the ladylike-minded who gather together at one another's commodious country houses for a morning's workout with the golden boy with brunch thrown in and followed by chardonnay, gossip and unrequited pinings.

All of which would be a recipe for disaster if their husbands found out except for one teeny tiny detail; being, of course, that Caspar is gayer than a regiment of hussars and camper than a California trailer park. So that's all right then. He can spend all morning criticising their seats, telling them to pull their shoulders back and really get those chests out

(like he'd care if they did) and shoving his whacker through their bra straps to stiffen their spines. And they can canter about harbouring dark thoughts about White Stuff and spend the afternoon debating whether a frantic few minutes in a loose box would harden or soften Caspar's attitudes. And so on and so forth.

The point being that, actually, no one has ever actually tried so much as a half-pass in earnest at Caspar. So no one is really, certainly sure. Which just adds to the excitement. Because Caspar really does have a way with horses and when he gets into the saddle – steady! – his mounts –steady now! – respond to his gentle instruction – STEADY! – by performing – *STEADY!* – the most complex movements!

You can take a horse to water but who really knows which side of the trough he prefers?

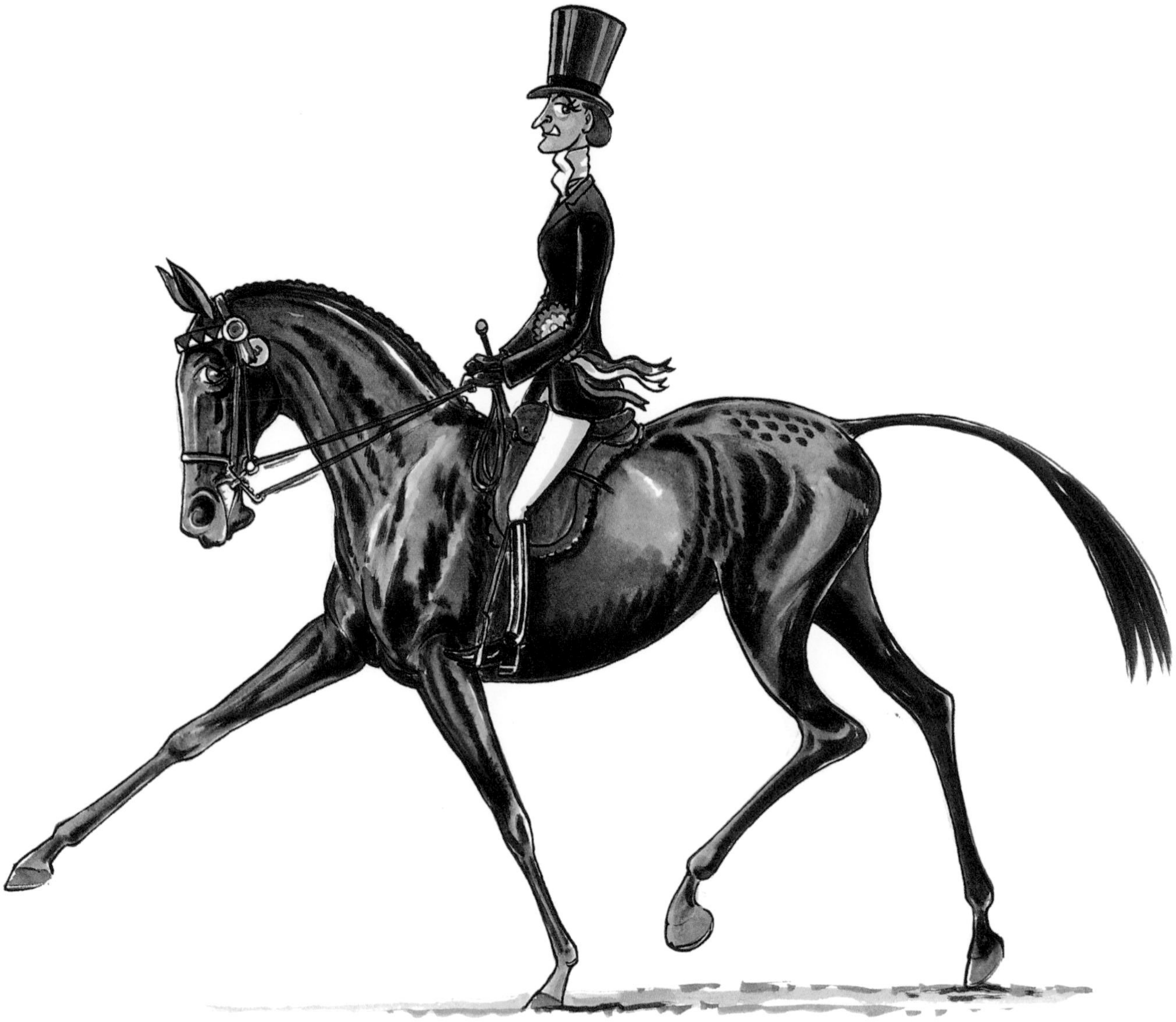

SHOWING...OFF

CROSS COUNTRY

VERY CROSS COUNTRY

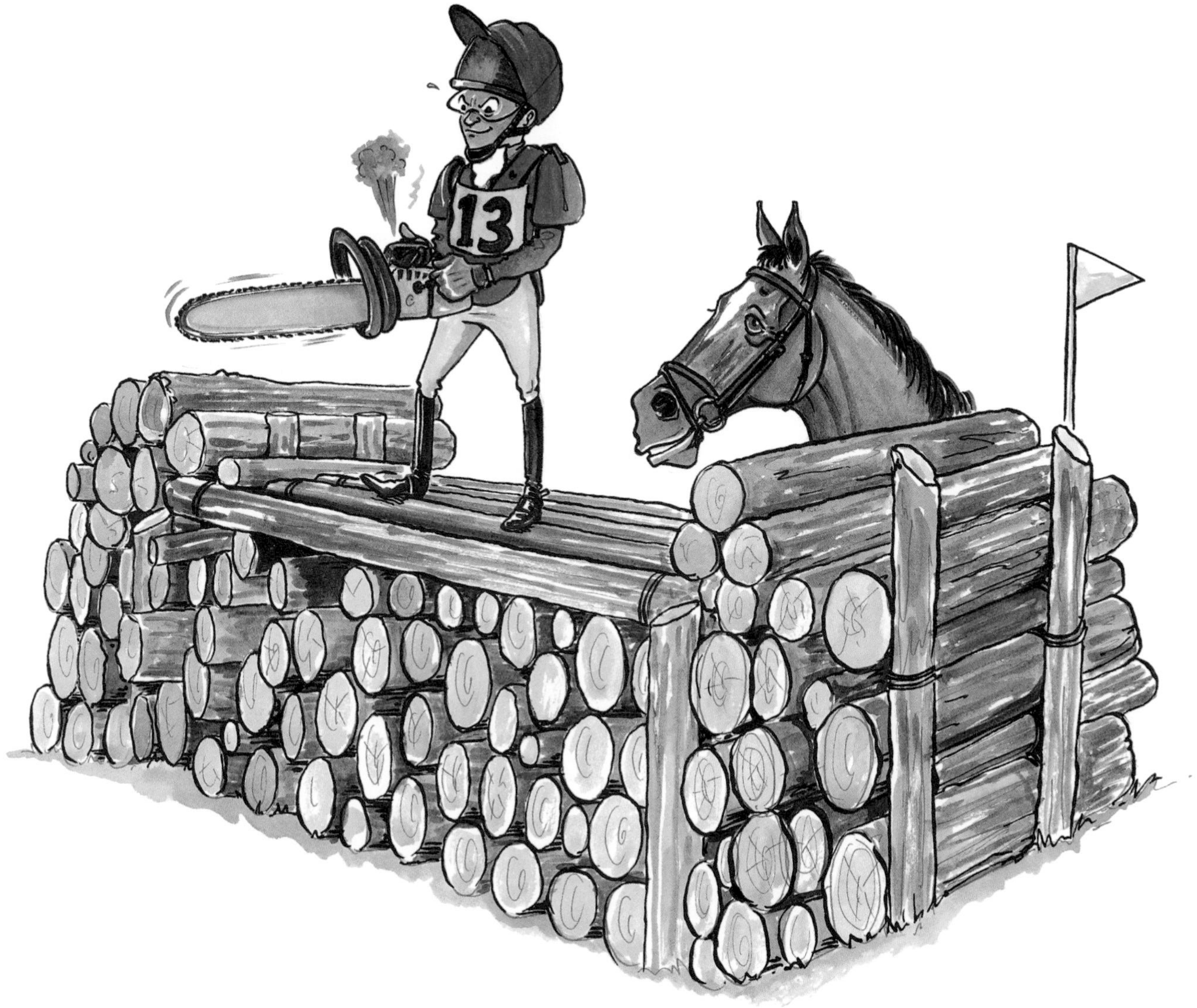
13

Clearing the Course

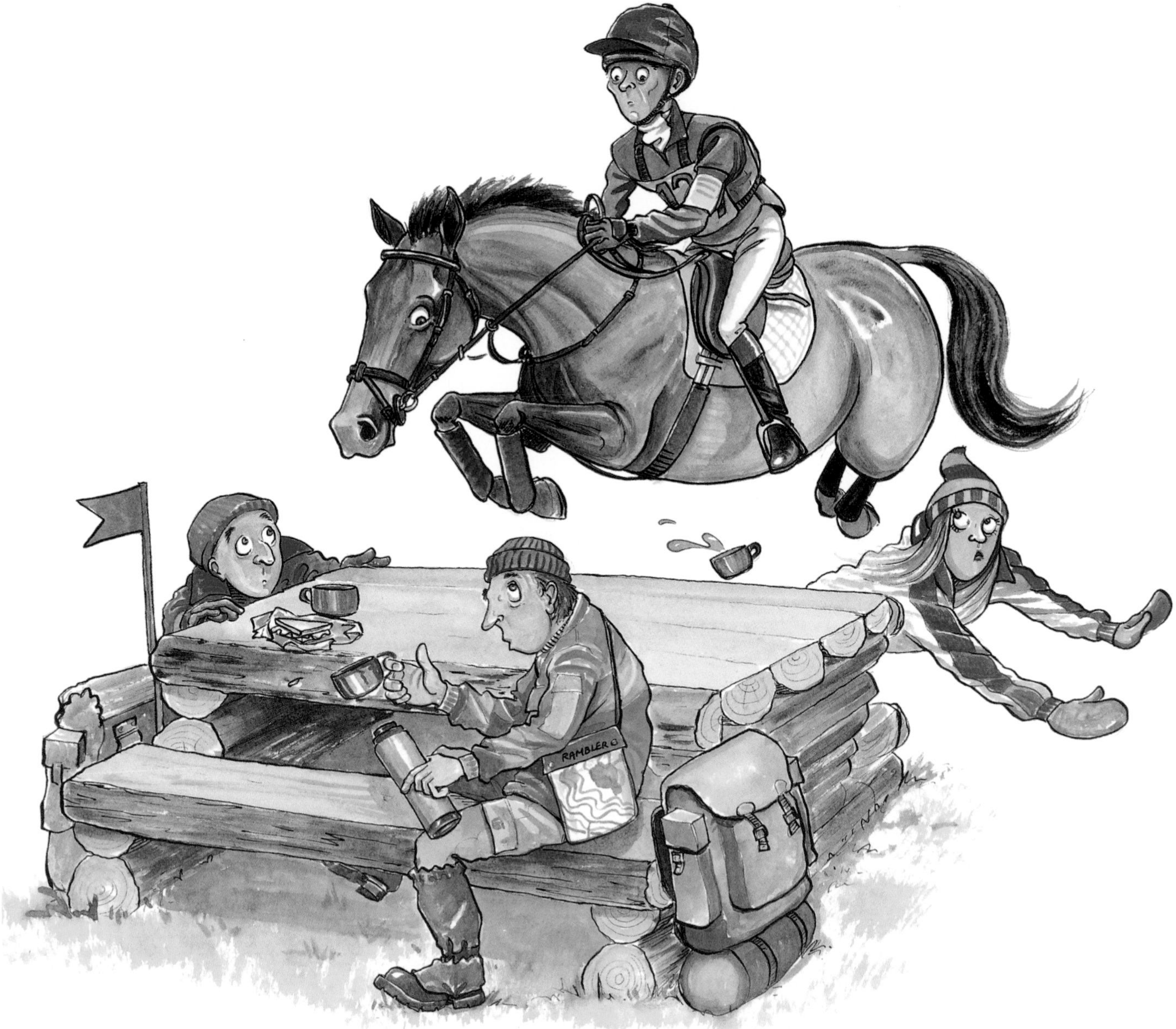
RAMBLER

The Picnic Table

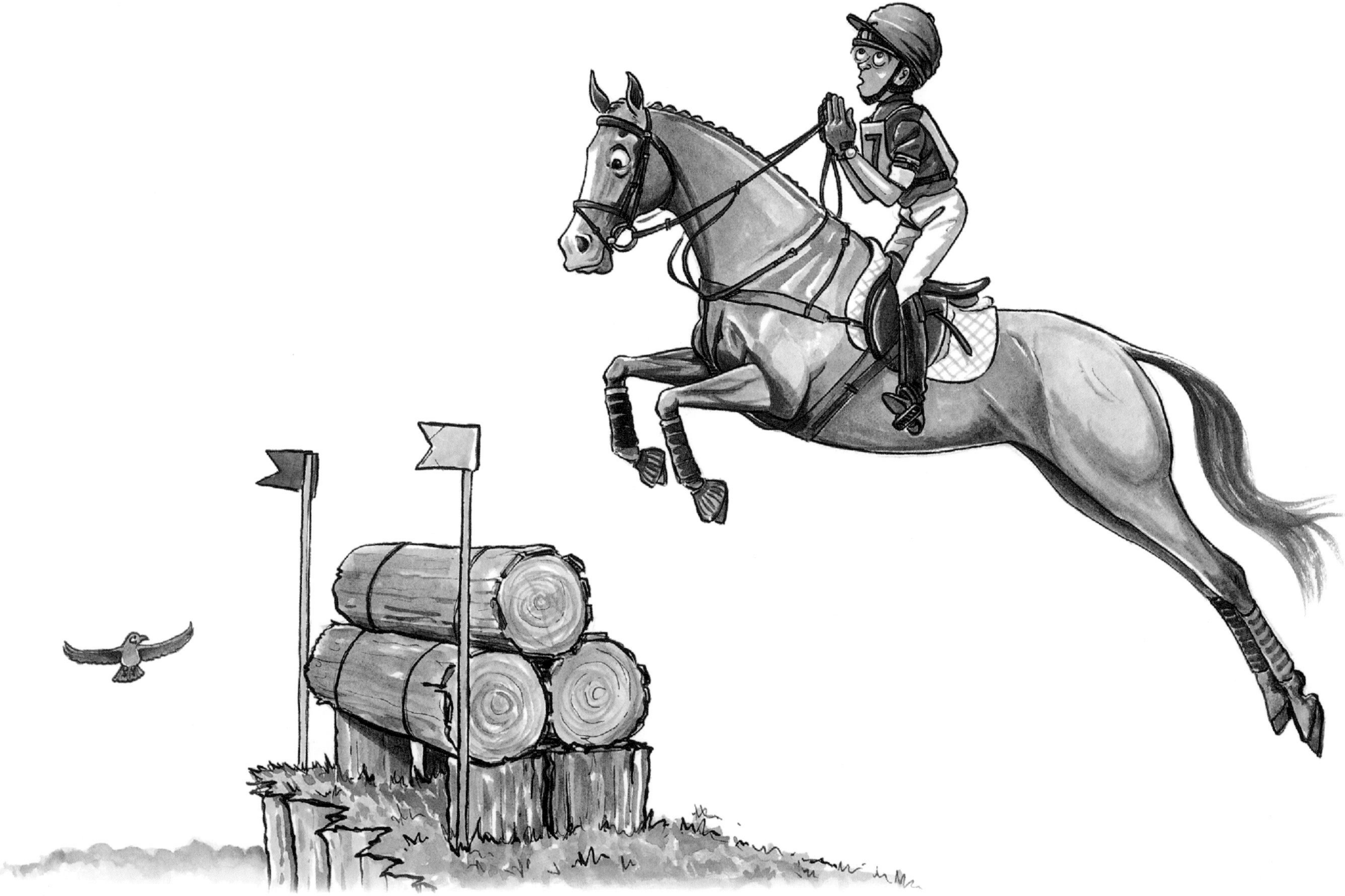
7

Wing and a Prayer

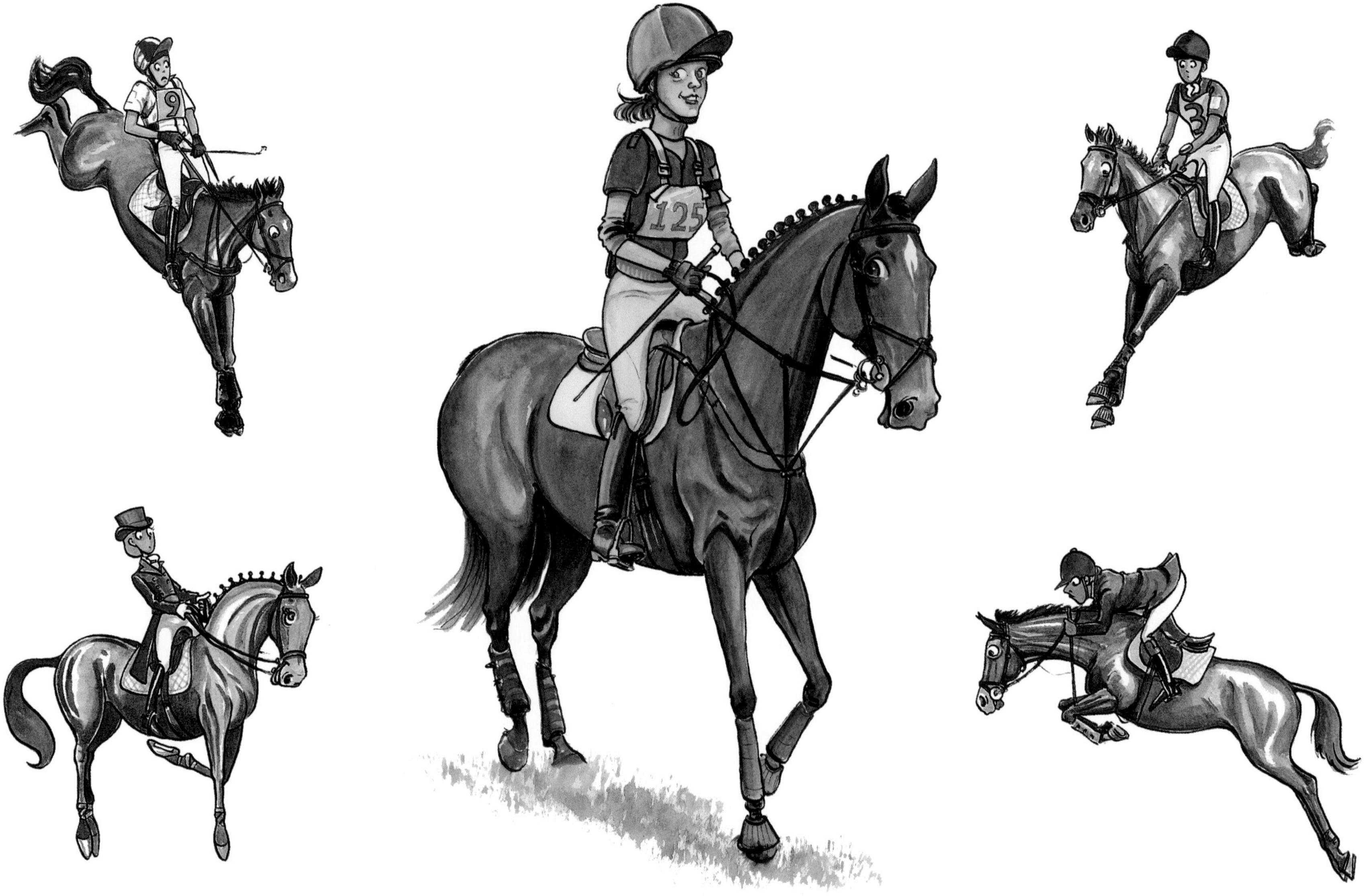
9
125
3

THE THREE DAY EVENTER

She's on the cusp. She has all the skills. She has been riding seriously for a decade. She has the iron self control which is central to flawless dressage. She can read her way round a cross-country course as if she had the designer on a short leash with her pointing out the traps and the pitfalls and the shortcuts and escape routes which have been surreptitiously embedded in every jump. She can calculate the paces round a showjumping arena to the half inch and can sense when her horse is about to put in a shorty and will pick him up bodily and heft him over the fence herself by main force if needs be. At just eighteen she has the physical strength and the stamina to hold her, their, performance together over a gruelling long weekend. She's paid her dues and taken her lumps. Most particularly, she has, as any number of judges, trainers and fellow competitors have repeated over the years, the key element which is the sign of true potential as surely as if it were branded on her forehead. She can communicate with horses. She has the wavelength. That instinctive connection that makes a horse give that little bit extra at the crucial moments, to shave

tenths off a time or to flick its heels over the last pole of the last double and which turns mere luggage into a true rider and which given time, training and a decent mount and a dose of luck, could make her a champion. If she wants it enough.

Enough to sacrifice the rest. The parties and the holidays are small things. Commitment to achieving equestrian greatness involves much more than missing out on a few jollies. It means devoting the rest of your life to the pursuit of excellence in the narrow furrow that is three-day eventing. Every waking minute. And that's just for the training of horses and rider. The rest of the day must be given over to scaling the Himalayan hurdle of funding the whole ludicrously expensive exercise. Which means finding and keeping sponsors. And coping with the gaping black holes in the accounts when sponsors fail, collapse, go broke, go mad or just simply change their minds and decide

to back someone else. Then there are horses to find, beg, borrow. Spotting them isn't easy, beating off the competition isn't easy, bringing them on isn't easy, keeping them fit isn't easy and winning on them is next to impossible. The biggest rostrum in the world still only holds three people and there are hundreds jostling for a spot. Jostling? Fighting. Tooth and nail. And outside of the spotlight there are plenty more trying to get in. Training hard, working the clock round, drumming up the cash and failing in droves through no fault of their own.

And the time to make the decision is now. This year's college and university courses are filling up fast and if you want to be a doctor or a lawyer or a nurse or a therapist or a manicurist or a plumber you had better get your skates on and your forms in or the moment is gone. Which is it to be? The rest of your life starts here. Right now. You have to choose.

If you walk around the lorry parks in the quiet of a summer's evening it's not unusual to hear girls crying into their horses necks. That's the sound of dreams dying.

61

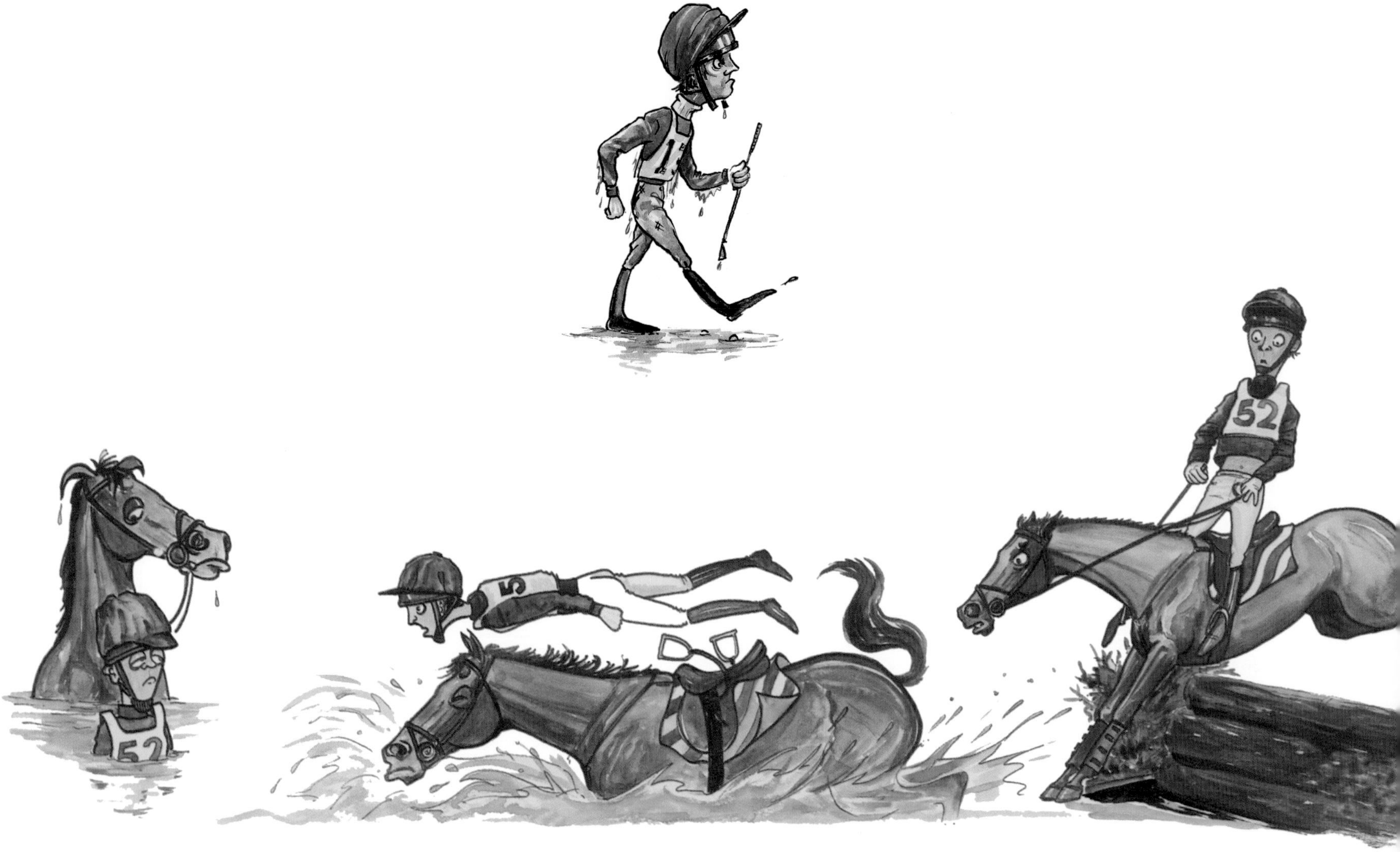
5
52

The Water Jump

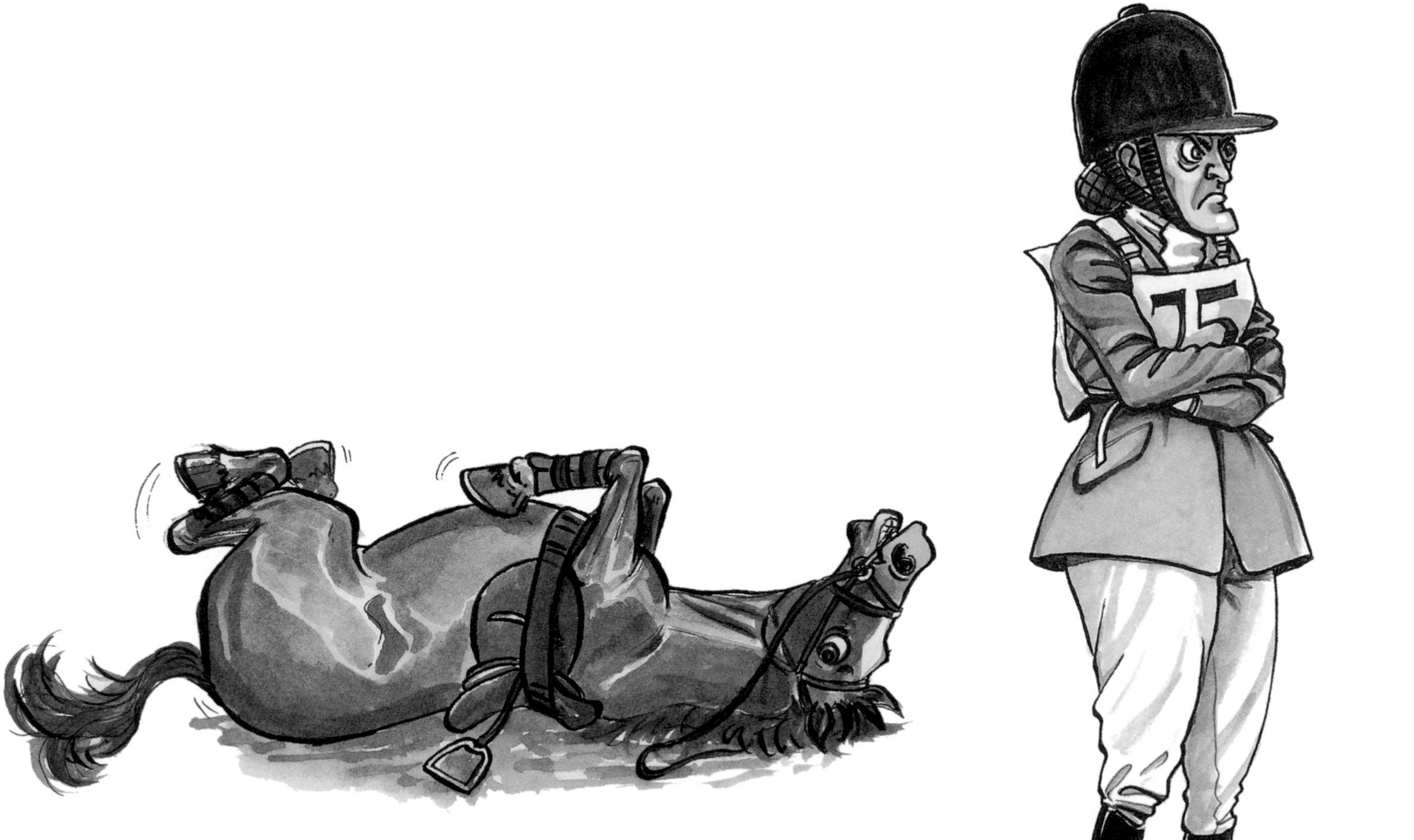
75

THE JUDGE'S DECISION IS FINAL

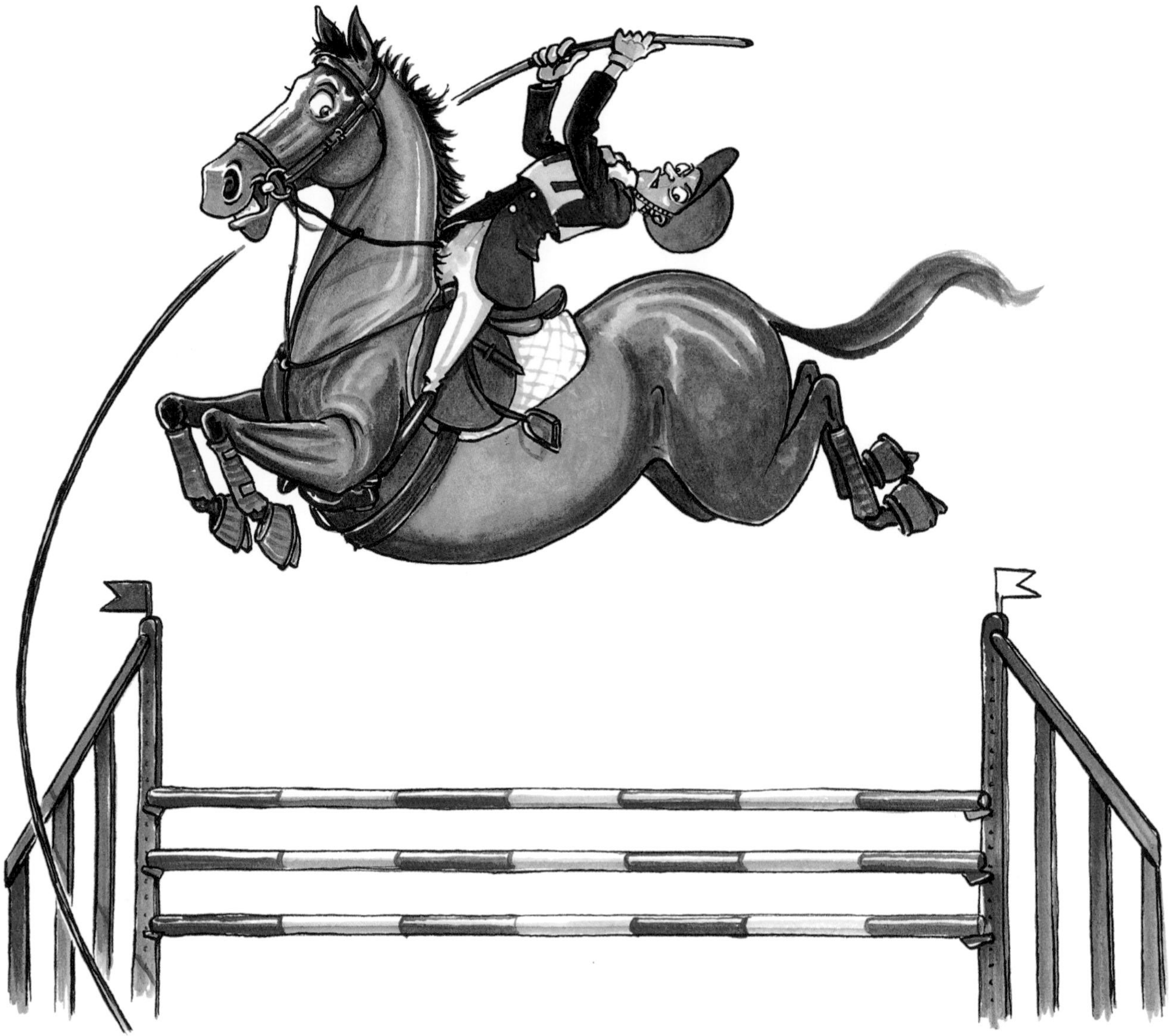

Clearing The Pole

SHOW JUMPING

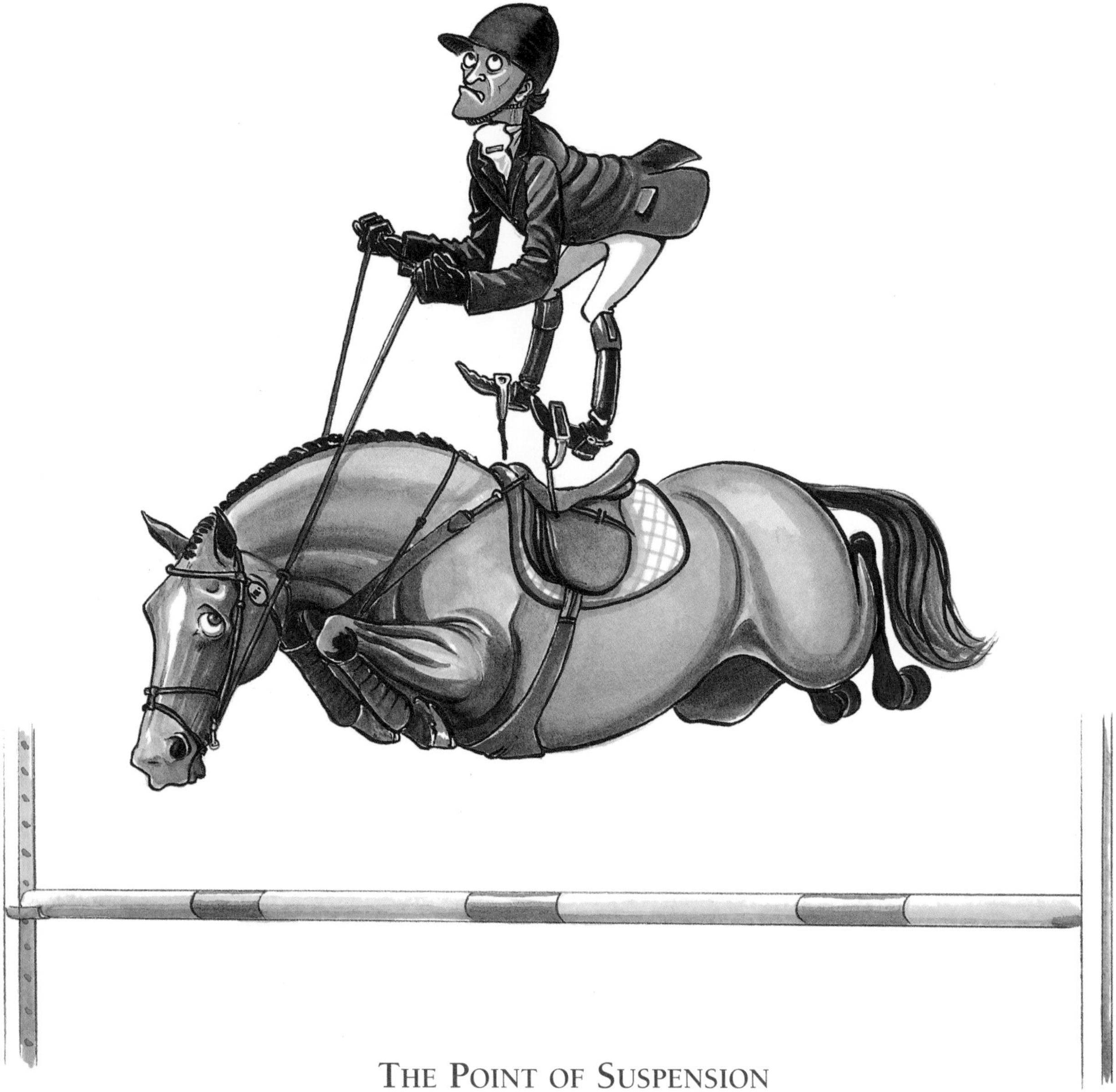

THE POINT OF SUSPENSION

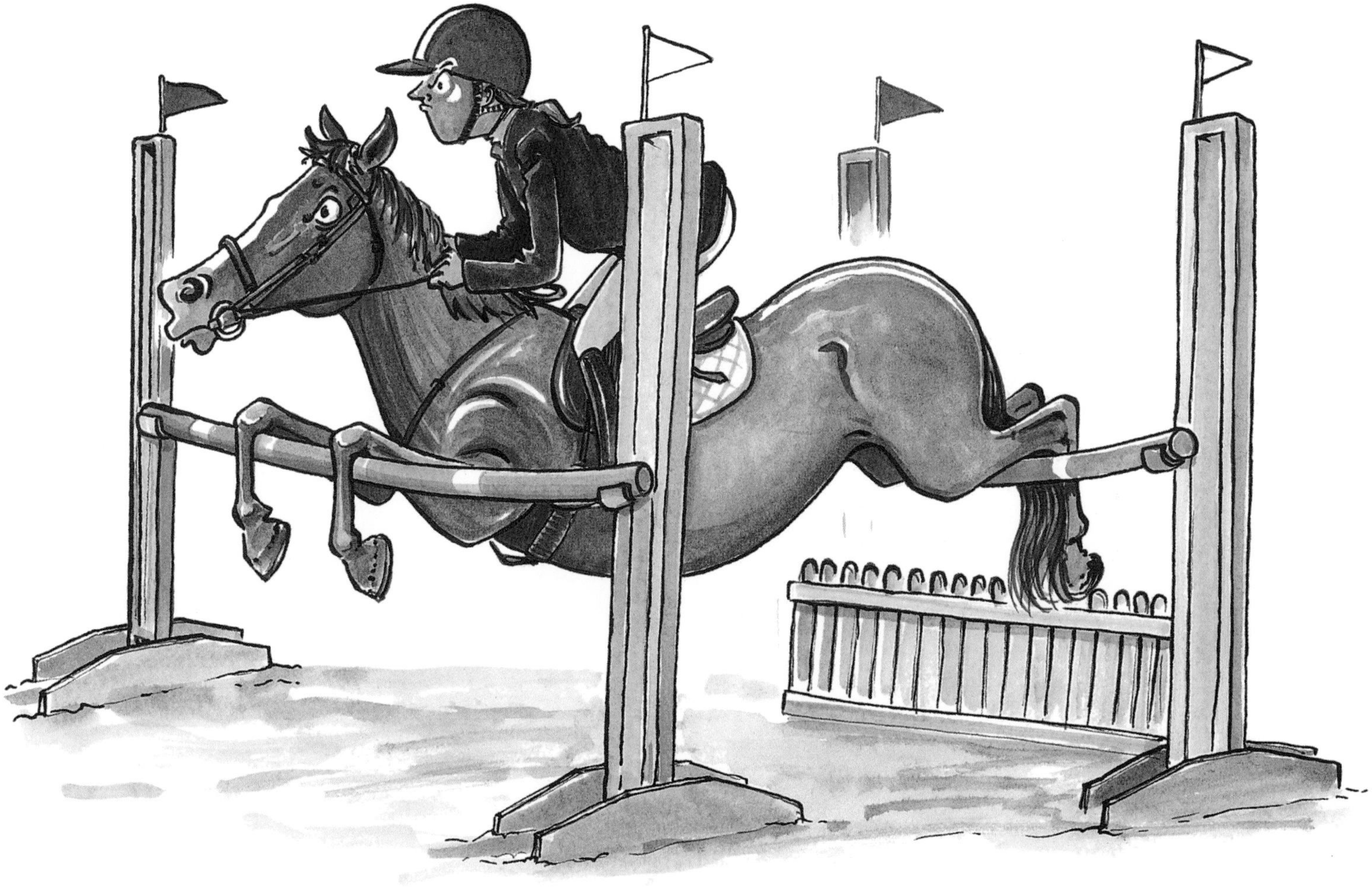

Suspended

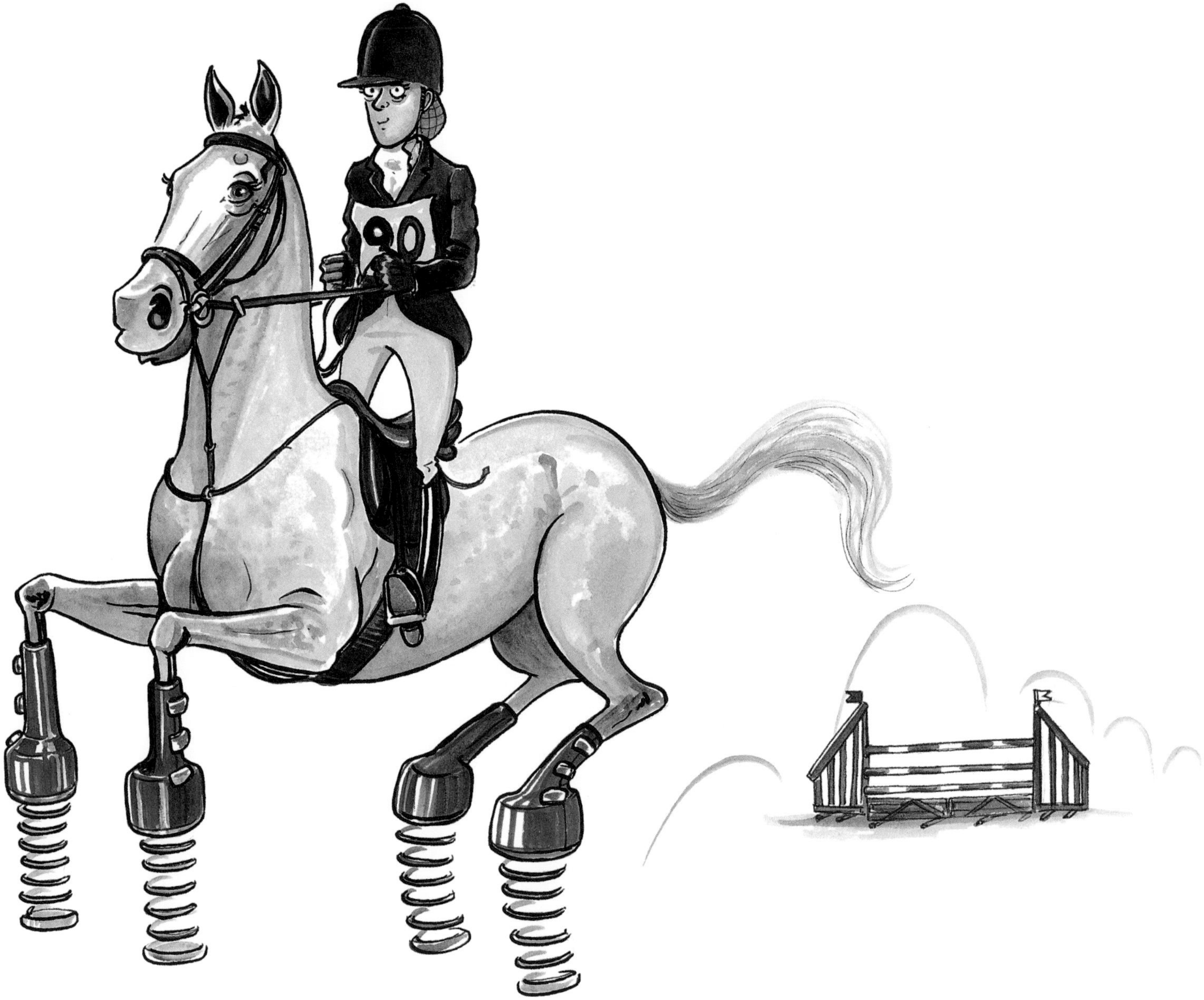
90

HIGHLY SPRUNG

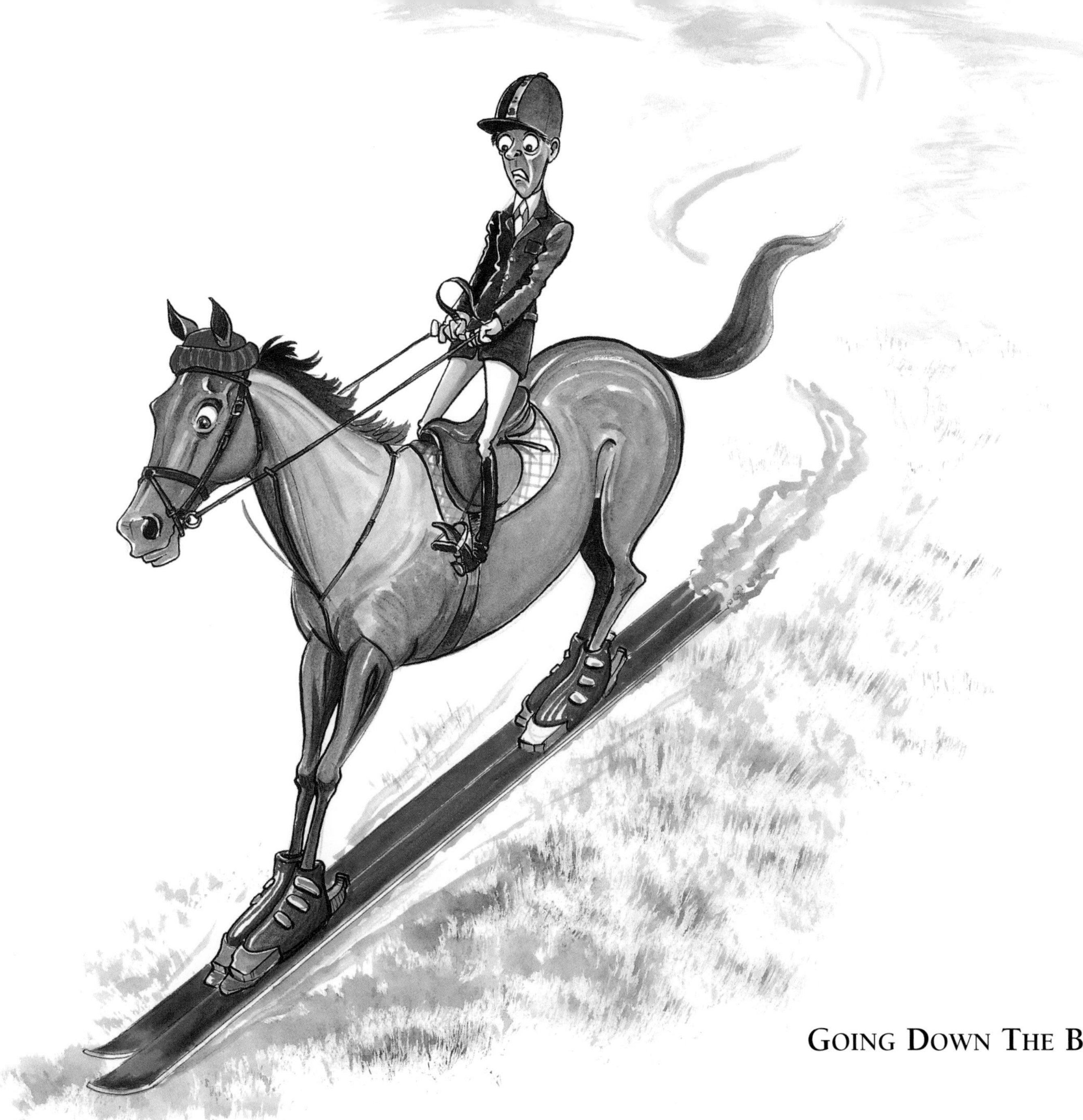

Going Down The Bank

RACING...over the sticks

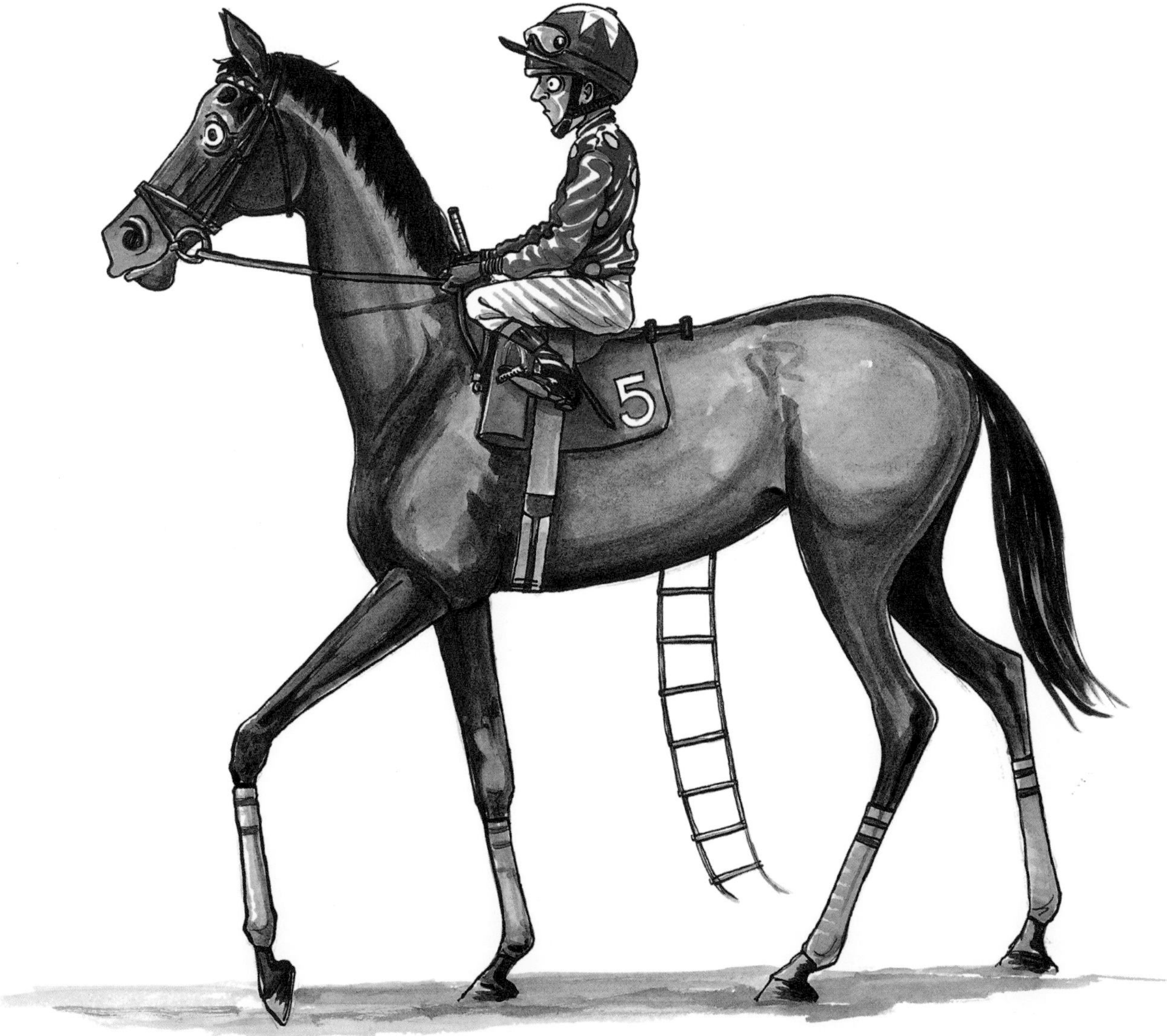
5

THE HIGH HORSE

THE GROOM

The groom is young and pretty and thin and cold. She's young because if you want to climb the greasy pole to anywhere near the top of the equestrian tree you have to start early. She's pretty because she's still young enough for the groom's gruelling lifestyle to polish rather than dull her unaffected beauty. She's thin because the groom's work is hard and her diet dubious. She's cold because the groom's day starts early; in the dark early; winter and summer. First there are the in-horses to rug up and turn out and their boxes to muck out. Then the out-horses must be checked and fed. Then the morning ride horses must be brought in and fed, unrugged, groomed and tacked up and put on the walker for an hour. After which there is a moment for breakfast of tea and bacon sandwiches. Then sweep the yard and do as much admin. – farriers' appointments, vet's calls, food orders – as time will allow before it is time to ride out. Take the horses off the walker. Others may arrive to ride out but more than likely the groom will have to exercise more than one herself. This will take her through the rest of the morning when there will be a pause for more tea and sandwiches. Then it will be back to riding out again in the afternoon after which there will be two or three training sessions in the indoor school and perhaps a lesson to oversee and then the inside horses must be brought in again, de-rugged and re-rugged, fed and bedded before she can make a start on the tack cleaning. After which she can finish off the day's admin, drink more tea, eat more bacon sarnies and collapse in a heap. All day; everyday; week in, week out.

Until the season starts. Be it racing, hunting, eventing, show-jumping. And if it's not one it's the other. Which means that the horses, or some of them, must be brought in and de-rugged and washed and clipped and plaited and tacked up and re-rugged and bandaged and booted and loaded into the freshly MOT-ed lorry which must then be driven to the venue where they must be unloaded, unbooted and de-rugged and unbandaged and rebandaged and booted and then hunted. After which they are untacked and re-booted and re-loaded and driven home where they can be unloaded and debooted and unbandaged and washed off and re-rugged and fed and watered and bedded before feeding and watering and exercising the ones which were left behind and then she can clean the tack. And do more admin.

Once the season gets into full swing, life transfers pretty much completely into the lorry. Because for every outing the horses must be washed and groomed and plaited and bandaged and booted and loaded and driven to the other end of the country where they will be unloaded and unbooted and disbandaged and tacked up and warmed up and competed in a gruelling series of trials before being cooled off, rinsed down, fed and watered, re-booted and rebandaged and reloaded for the night during which they can be driven to another site where they can be unloaded and rested so that the next morning they can be fed and watered and unloaded and groomed and plaited again and warmed up for another series of competitions against much the same people as the day before yesterday after which they will be untacked, rinsed off, re-booted and loaded in time for the groom to scrub off and frock up in time to attend the concluding shindig at which all the grooms drink and dance and gossip until the wee small hours when they go back to their lorries to check on the horses before drinking more tea and eating enough sarnies to stay awake long enough to drive the lorry to the next venue.

And so it goes on. And on. And on. And on.

73

THE YARD DOG

Friday. Cold. Wet. Miserable. Didn't do much. Had breakfast. Lay in front of Aga for most of the morning. Taunted one of the cats. Cat scratched nose. Hate cat. Hoofed out after lunch for vigorous exercise on lead of all things. Slip collar just outside gate and return to Aga. Growl at cat. Cat hisses. Retreat under chair. Find old tennis ball under chair. Chew tennis ball. Tennis ball disintegrates. Scatter bits of tennis ball around kitchen floor. Vigorous exercise party return. 'Where the bloody hell have you been then? We've been looking high and low for you?.. Blah-blah-blah…damn good thrashing…blah-blah…one of these days…blah. Walk across kitchen holding one paw up. Pandemonium.

'Oh my god, he's hurt.' 'Hit by car…rush to vet…poor darling!' and more besides.

Good sport. Passes half an hour till they all come to their senses. Given supper by the fire. This is the life.

Saturday. Had breakfast. I like Saturdays. The children all turn up which means any number of treats. The yard is full of ponies. Nip ponies' heels. Ponies kick. Yah-boo sucks couldn't kick a fat old Labrador, let alone me. Nyah. Nyah. Nyah. They all go out riding so I mooch into the barn where the hay is kept. Brilliant! There's a rat in here somewhere. I know it.

Maybe a couple. Zoom round to the office barking like a mad bandit to find one of the girls having coffee. Eventually she gets the message – Duh! – and comes with me to the barn. I assume position.

She says 'What is it then?' like she doesn't know and picks up bale. Bingo! Things go a bit haywire. Rats run. Girl leaps about making strange noise. Got one. Bumph! Just like that. Crunch and done. The other one got under the door before I could reach him. Picked up rat and offered it to girl for her help. Didn't seem interested. Squeaked a bit. Walked through cattle yard and nipped a few heels for devilment. Spent afternoon by the Aga. Supper.

Grabbed cat's tail and ran like buggery. Met someone coming through door with tray. Bit of a shemozzle to be honest. Crashing sounds. Slipped out through cat-flap and spent the night in one of the looseboxes to be on the safe side.

Sunday. Back in through cat-flap to find breakfast already on boot room floor and Labradors about to help themselves. Give Labradors a bit of a talking to. Breakfast.

Down to the yard to say good morning to all the children and nip the ponies. Splendid! Follow the ride as far as the edge of big wood and then hive off to check out the fox earth. No one home by the scent of it, unless…Ooh er! Mr Brock the Badger. Tooo scary! Fortunately find fresh badger dung and roll in it thoroughly to be on the safe side before legging it home. Reception not good. Herded firmly into yard and then tied up with binder twine and hosed – hosed, moi! – for what seemed like hours. Then scrubbed with awful stuff and HOSED again. And she never stopped shouting the whole time. Dun'no what she's on about to be honest. S'only poo. Finally released.

Lie in sun on mounting block for a while. V. V. fluffy and highly scented. Cross the clover field to try my luck with the bitch across the way. She's looking lovely as ever and is hot to be pushed to St Neots ivunowaddamean. Can't get into blasted run before huge bloke comes roaring up with business-like looking stick. Blow cutes a kiss goodbye and make tracks.

Spend afternoon by Aga. Supper. Chewed some socks.

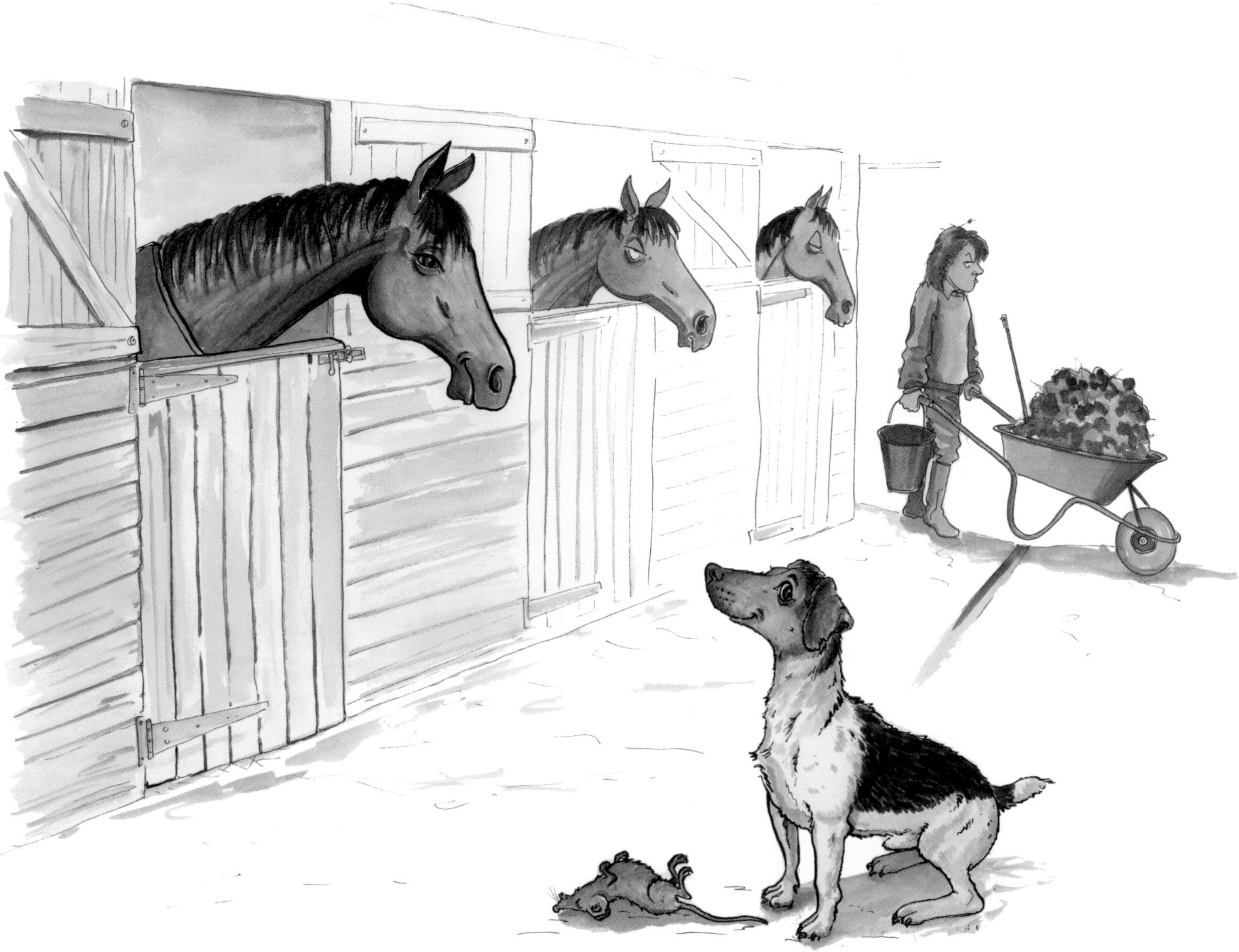

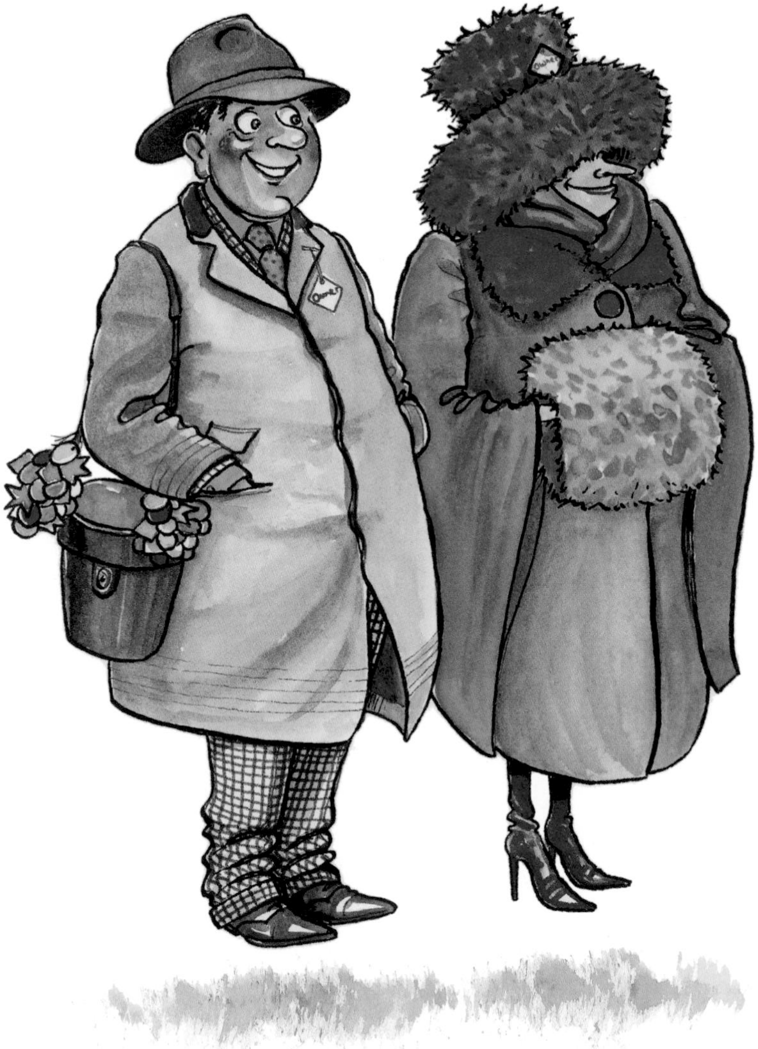

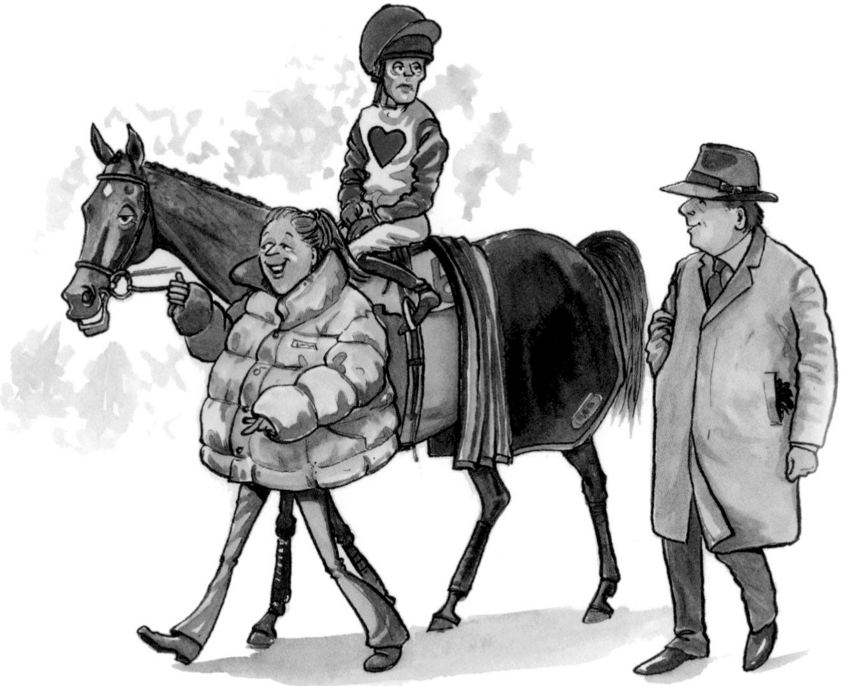

THE OWNERS

It's not Ascot and its not Ladies' Day. In fact it's a good deal further north and about fifteen degrees colder, but for the owners who have come to see their sweetheart run it could be the Royal Enclosure and that's a fact.

He is resplendent in double-breasted houndstooth and racing felt. From his binoculars case dangle a positive bunting of multi-coloured badges from meetings up and down the country. Only one however dangles from his lapel 'Owner.' It gets him into the grandstand; it gets him into the paddock. It gets him everywhere. And he just loves it.

She is in muted shades but plenty of them. There is a heather mixture twinset over a lilac cashmere lurking under the voluminous mauve cloak and a pink pashmina somewhere to highlight the ruby earrings which are invisible under her broad fur hat. A scarlet stripe of lipstick divides hat from cape and gives the onlooker a clue as to the direction she is facing. But at least she's warm.

And they are thrilled to be here and so terribly excited as they are led by their trainer – their trainer – into the paddock to meet their jockey – their jockey – before the canter down to the start. They pat the horse and they pat the jockey and they pat the trainer and they pat the horse again for luck and make their way back to the rails by the finish so that they can be absolutely sure of seeing him romp home.

And at the off he's a bit boxed in but as the field finds the pace he's holding his own as they go out of sight down the far side of the course but as they re-appear after the fifth he's still there with the pack although there are several strung out now behind them. One of the leaders goes at the sixth which leaves him lying third as they pound past the finish for the first time. And the owners are doing their collective nut. Houndstooth is jumping up and down in a fluorescent rainbow of bouncing badges and the missus is flapping like a great mauve bat with her hat over her eyes. As the runners disappear below the brow again there is another faller and for a heartstopping moment the commentator is uncertain but…it…wasn't him and now he's second as they start the long climb up the hill and they can barely contain themselves because all he's got to do is hang on and not stumble or unseat his jockey – their jockey – and they're in the frame for the first time and at the last it's the leader who catches the last hurdle and almost goes on landing but staggers on and so as they come to the run in he's actually in front – 'HE'S IN FRONT!! HE'S IN FRONT!' and as they pass the line a racing felt and a broad fur hat fly briefly aloft above a blur of dancing mauve and bold checks. And in the winner's enclosure – the winner's enclosure! – the jockey jumps down to be congratulated by his owners – owners – and the owners pat the horse and pat the jockey and hug the trainer and kiss each other and to the rest of the world it may only be the Benefield PVC Replacement Windows Handicap Hurdles but to the owners it's the Arc and the National rolled into one and it's theirs. Their horse. Their trophy. Their mantelpiece. They own it.

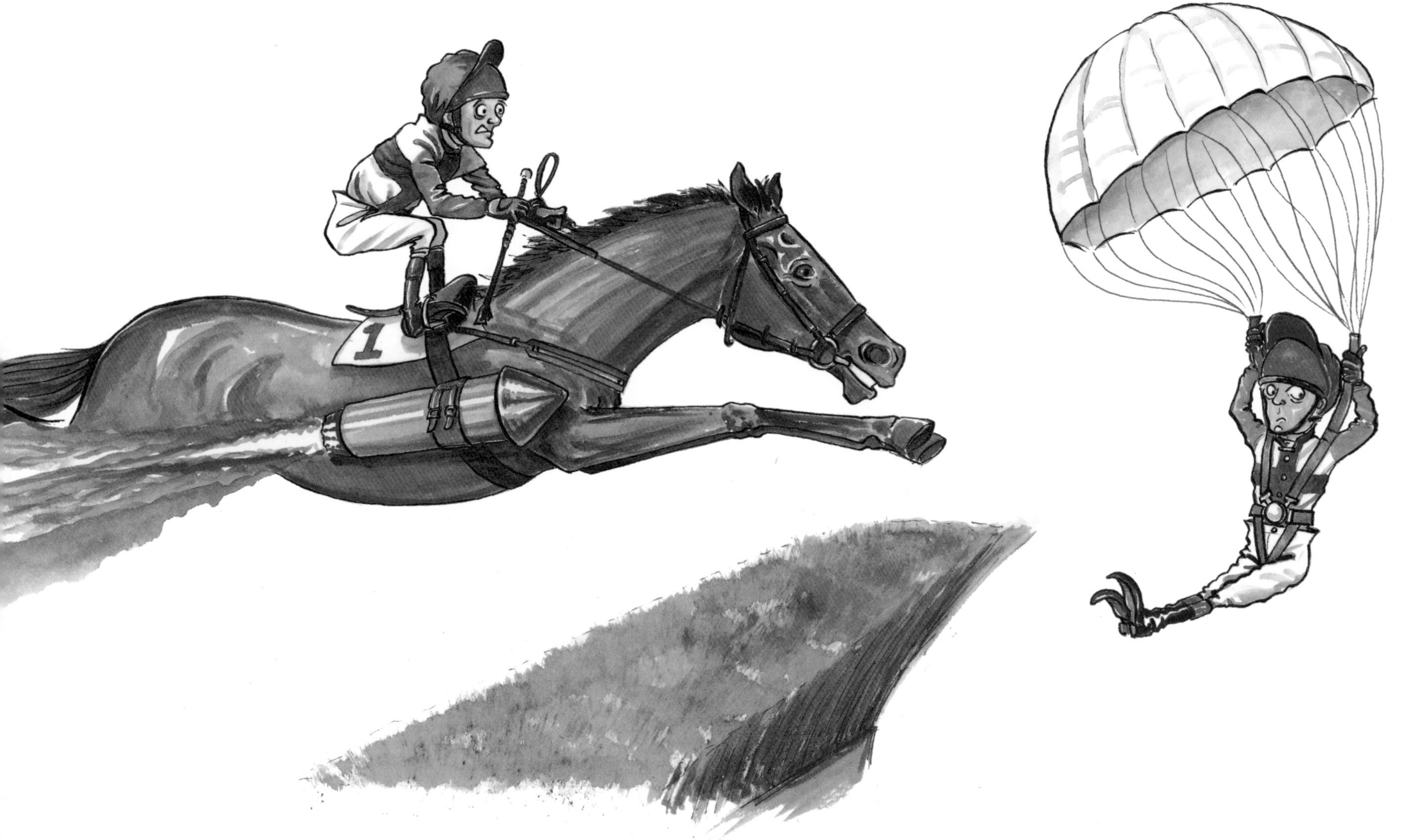
1

Rocket Propelled

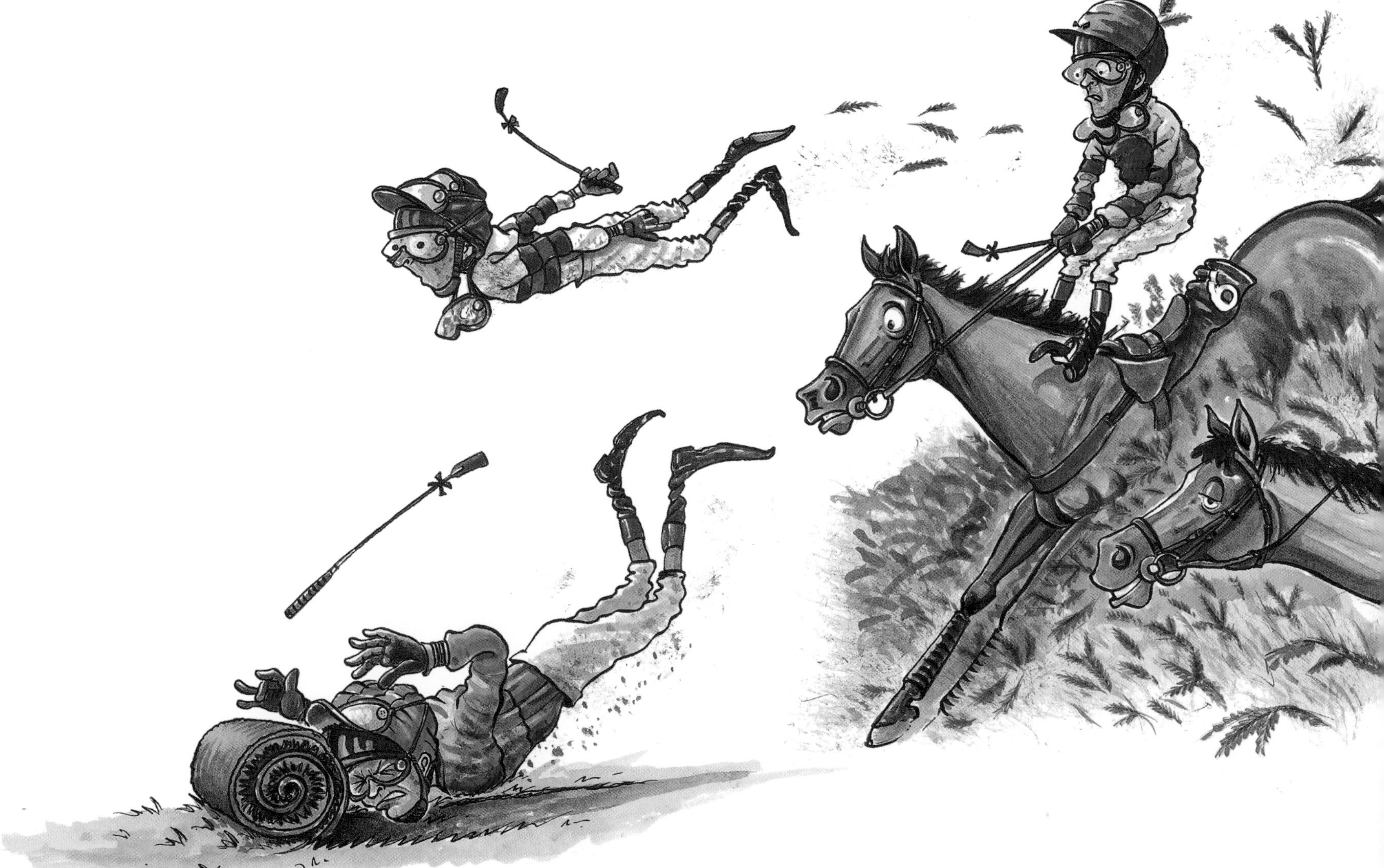

The Turf Club

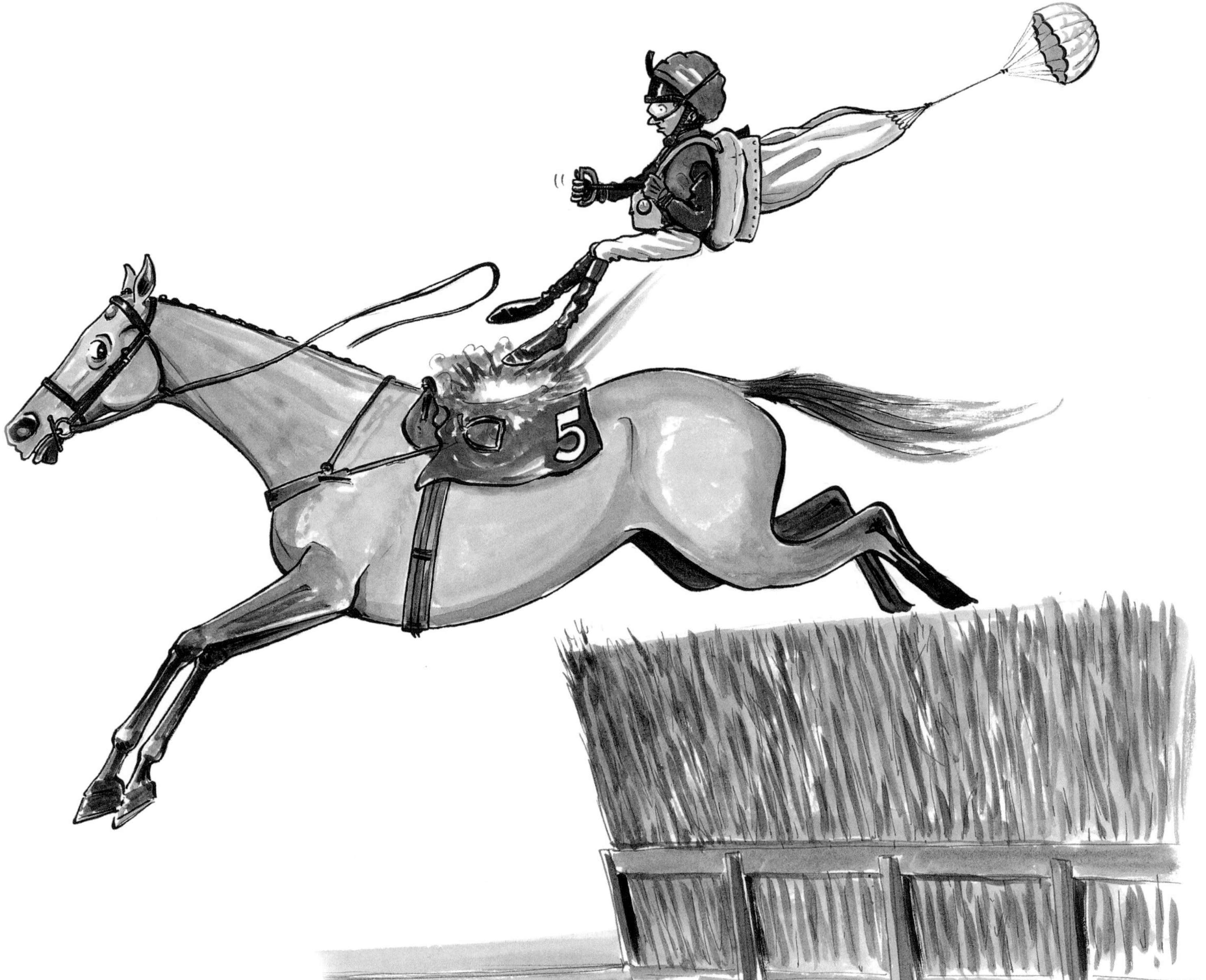
5

THE EJECTOR SEAT

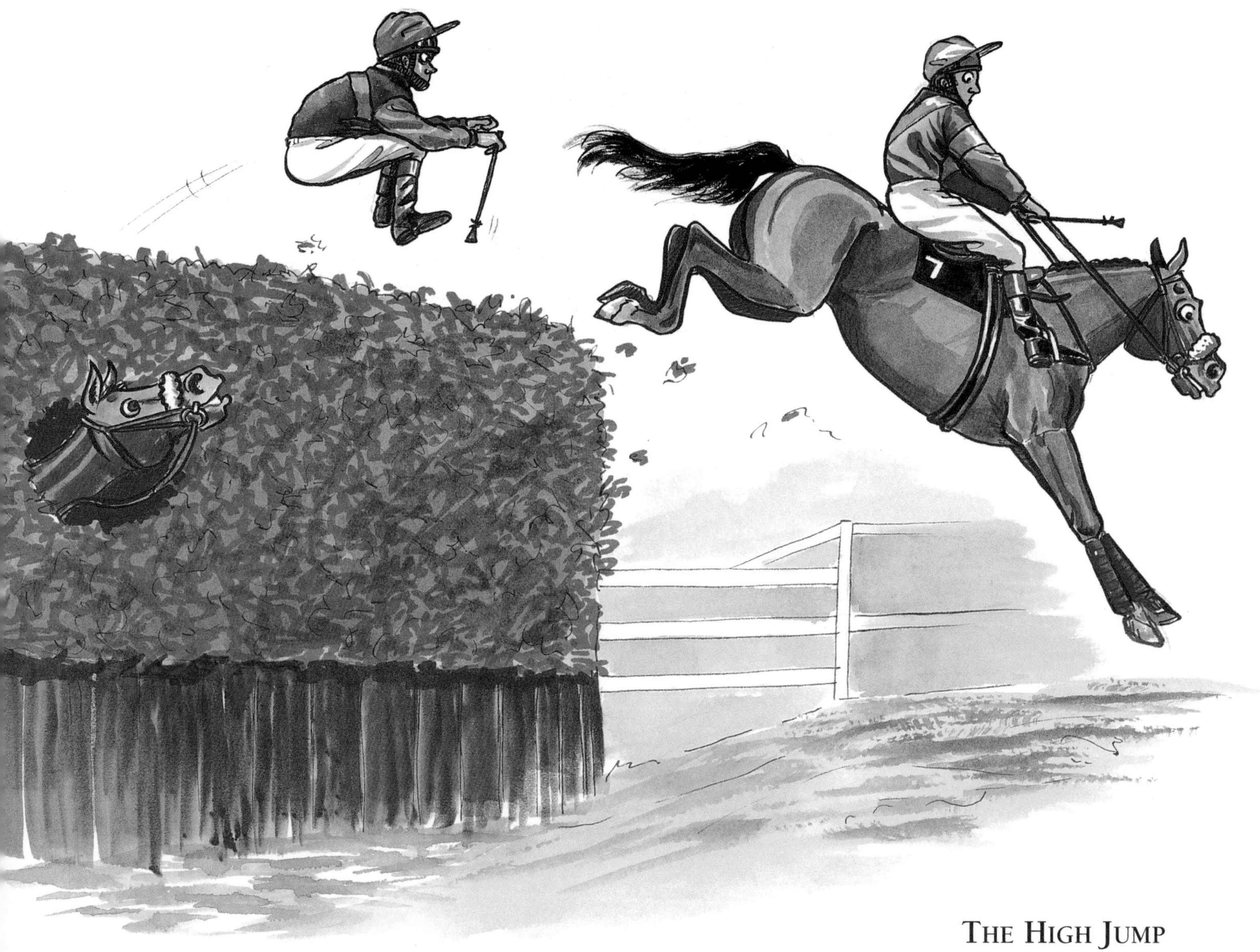
7

The High Jump

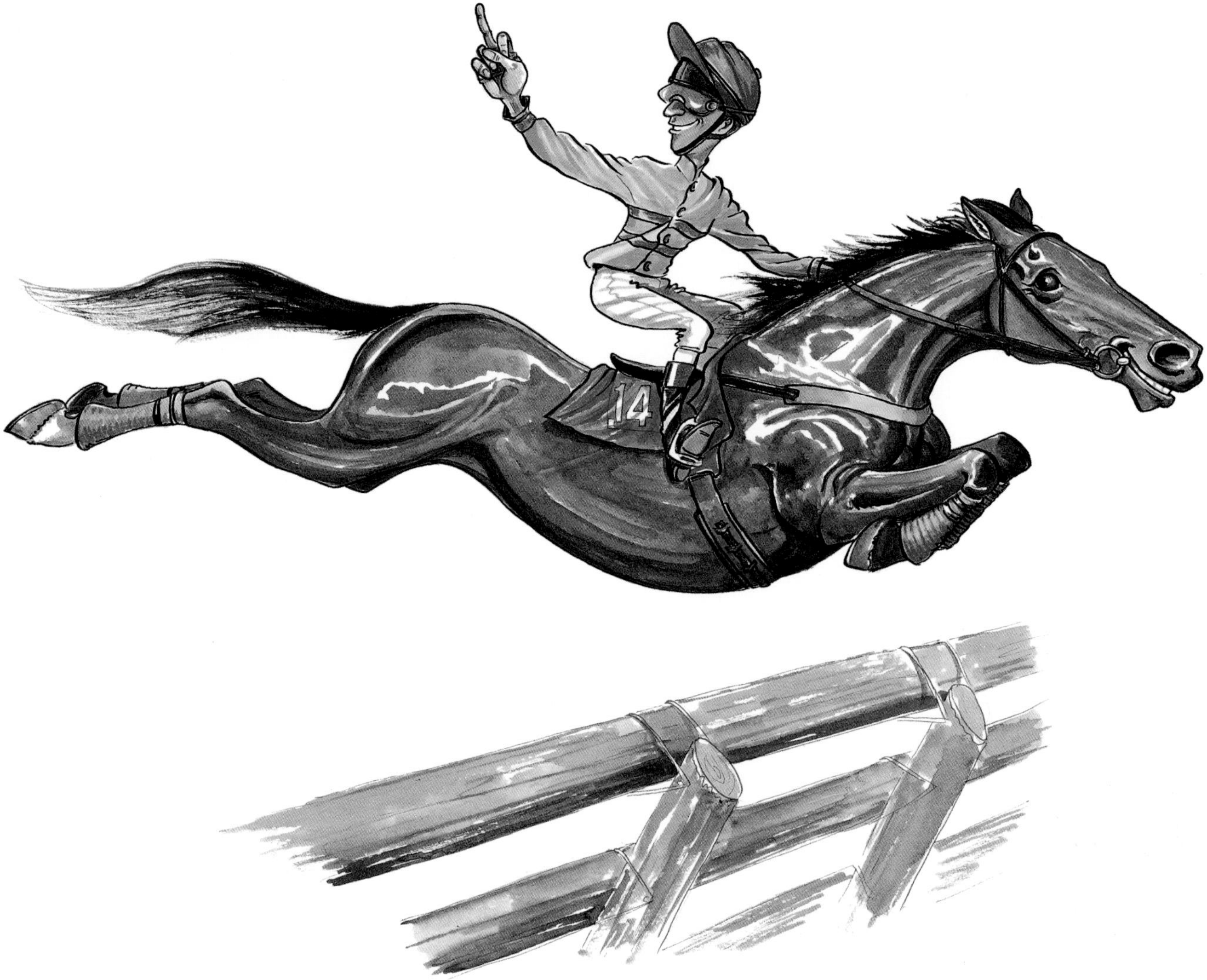
14

The Saluter

JOCKEYS

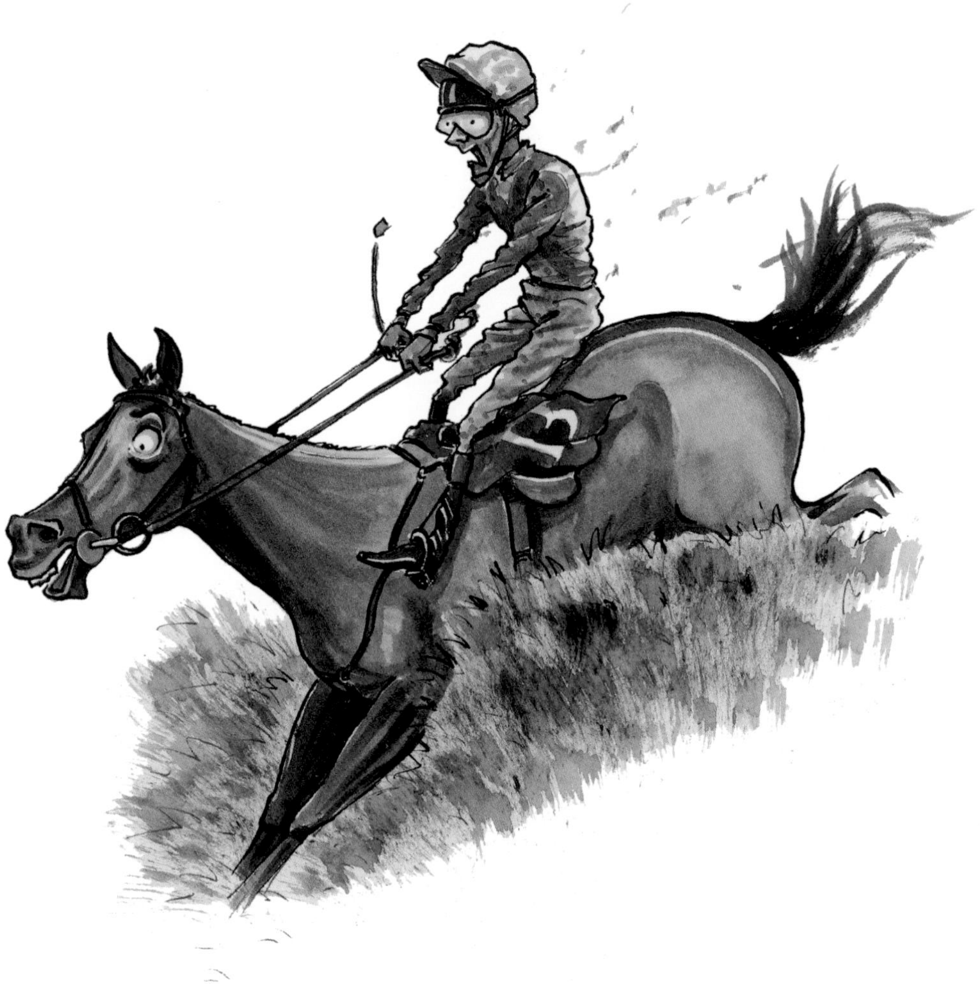

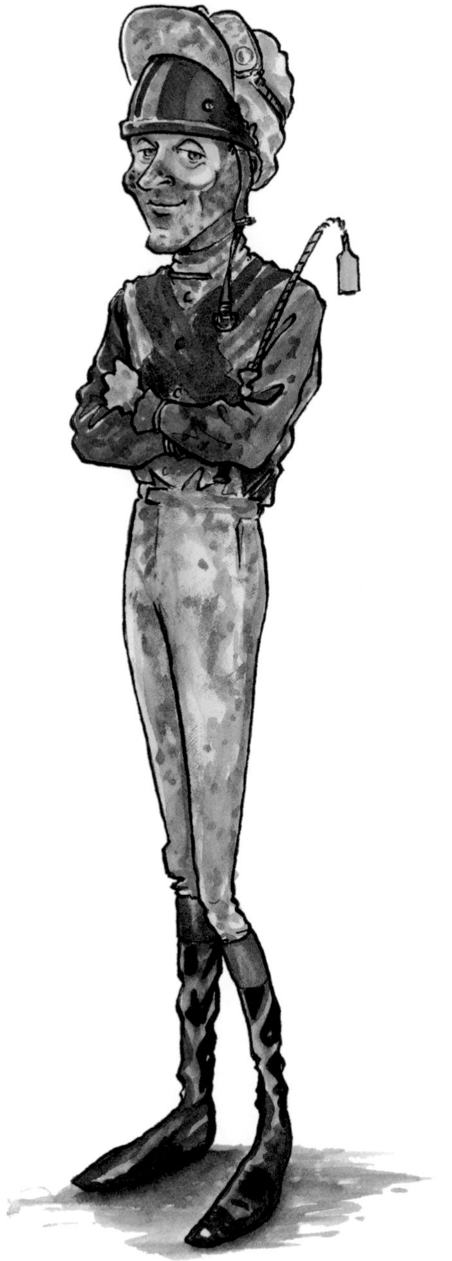

THE POINT-TO-POINTER

'Er… which way to the weighing room?' Rupert has a broad gap where his front teeth used to be before he took an early dismount at the fourth a couple of years back. He also has a permanent limp as the result of a bit of a moment two seasons ago, which left him with a nasty compound fracture and no ligaments flat in his left knee. What was really galling though was they insisted on cutting his boot off. Brand new boot too, dammit. Rupert has a slightly faraway look which is partly because he hasn't eaten anything but Jaffa cakes and black tea for the last week to make the weight and partly because he has had a slightly faraway look ever since he came off in a shemozzle after his stirrup leather broke as he was challenging for third coming to the last and didn't wake up for a week. He made the jump, or at least he made the take-off, but lost it on arrival and duly left by the side exit. Which also involved his collarbone – again – which still gives him a bit of gyp in the cold weather. Rupert is a point-to-point jockey.

He got the bug when he was in the Army. The Army was just nuts for him. There didn't seem to be much purpose in going to college because there wouldn't be very much fun and Rupert was never the sharpest tool in the box anyway so college would really only have been rubbing it in. The Army, on the other hand, or rather the Cavalry, offered everything Rupert could wish for. Polo all summer, skiing all winter and plenty of hunting in between. He spent the rest of his time roaring around the tank training areas of Germany in the turret of a Challenger running over the occasional Lada by day and roaring round the seedier parts of Hamburg in his Golf Gti and bumping into more Ladas by night.

When he came out he did a stint at agricultural college. Less though for the finer points of four course crop rotation than the continuation of a lifestyle which consisted largely of more polo, more hunting and more beer. And after that he really did have to come home and drive the tractor for a bit. Which he did, and does. But in between there is the hunting; which Rupert enjoys as much as ever. But hunting these days is not the adrenalin rush that it used to be. Not least because there is the rest of the field to consider and there are children on ponies and the bunch of namby-pambies loitering about at the back who want all the gates opened and are constantly looking for ways round the open ditches and see a good thick blackthorn hedge as an insuperable obstacle rather than a challenge. So for a straight forward, no holds barred, flat out from start to finish, up and at 'em, head down charge Rupert turned to point-to-pointing.

He rides his own horses and the horses of a few friends whom he has cajoled into a syndicate. Sometimes he even manages to finish somewhere towards the front which gives his friends a frisson of pride of ownership but which means nothing to Rupert for whom the ride is everything, plummeting into the ground a regular event and finishing in the saddle is a distinct, if occasional, bonus.

He's too tall by half and is in a constant state of malnutrition from trying to make the weight and it's a known fact that it will probably kill him in the end but he'll do it until hell or the course freezes over or something else happens that Rupert can't quite now remember. 'Er…where did you say the weighing room was again?'

THE JOCKEY

'Eis a good 'orse though. A bloody good 'orse. I knew 'e was a good 'orse the minute the boss brought 'im in the yard as a two year old. 'Is dam were a good 'orse, an' all, an' 'is sire, of course, was a bloody good 'orse as everyone knows. So I knew 'e was a good 'orse from the off. An' as 'e came on I was watchin' 'im an' I said to the boss, I said "'E's a bloody good 'orse, Boss." you know, 'an the boss said to me, you know, 'e said to me "'E is a good 'orse. A bloody good 'orse." So I knew then that 'e was a good 'orse. So I said to the boss, I said, you know, I said "Boss, that's a bloody good 'orse. When you want to put 'im in the stalls, I'd like to be up because 'e's a bloody good 'orse."'

'An' the boss said to me, 'e said, you know, 'e said "You can 'ave that ride when I put him in the stalls because I know you know a good 'orse when you see one. An' that's a bloody good 'orse."'

'So when 'e was ready the boss put 'im in a couple of races at meets about the place, but I didn't get the ride then because we didn't want too many people to know what a good 'orse 'e was at that time. So the boss 'e, you know, give the ride to a couple of the other lads so's that not too many people would know what a good 'orse 'e was. An' the lads said to the boss after, you know, they said "Boss, 'e's a good 'orse. 'E's a bloody good 'orse."'

'An' the boss said to me, you know, the lads thought that 'orse were a bloody good 'orse 'an I said to 'im, you know, "'E is a good 'orse.' 'Cos 'e is a good 'orse.

So we knew 'e was a good 'orse an' when the boss put 'im in for this race, 'e said to me, you know, like, this is a big race an' the 'orse 'as got a good chance at it 'cos 'e's a good 'orse an' so I want you up when 'e goes into the stalls 'cos you know 'e's a bloody good 'orse. An' I said "'E is a good 'orse, Boss, a bloody good 'orse."'

An' 'e said to me, 'e said, "Don't go daft at the off an' go harin' off like a daft thing, but keep 'im close to begin with and let the other daft buggers go harin' about. Jus' you keep him close or thereabouts and let 'im get the feel of the pace before you let 'im go because 'e's a good 'orse an' if you let 'im go early on 'e'll go, so don't you let him go, until the rest of 'em 'ave gone, an' then just about the turn, you know, when they've mostly gone, you let him go an' he'll go

and then you let 'im. An' he'll carry you home, you'll see, because 'e's a good 'orse."'

'So I held 'im in at first, you know, like the boss said, and let the others make the pace, you know, and just to let the 'orse get the feel of the pace, you know, an' 'e was enjoyin' himself no end, you know, an' 'e wanted to crack on, you know, but I held 'im back a bit on the rail, you know, like the boss said, an' let the others make the pace, you know, until the turn, an' then, you know, I give 'im a touch an' just moved 'im on a bit, an' 'e's such a good 'orse you know, 'e pushed on like a good 'un. An' I thought for a bit we might get boxed in as the others eased off, you know, but the old 'orse, 'e just looked at the gap, you know, and gather 'isself up and off 'e went. An' I did just show 'im the stick as we came down the run-in an' 'e never stopped runnin' till we was past the post, 'e was 'avin' such a grand time. Just lovin' it, 'e was, you know. But then, you know, 'e is a good 'orse. A bloody good 'orse.'

Not among the philosophical greats, perhaps, and few startling insights into the human condition. But you don't want anything much in your top jockey other than being a top jockey. And he is a good jockey. A bloody good jockey. And he knows a good horse when he sees one too.

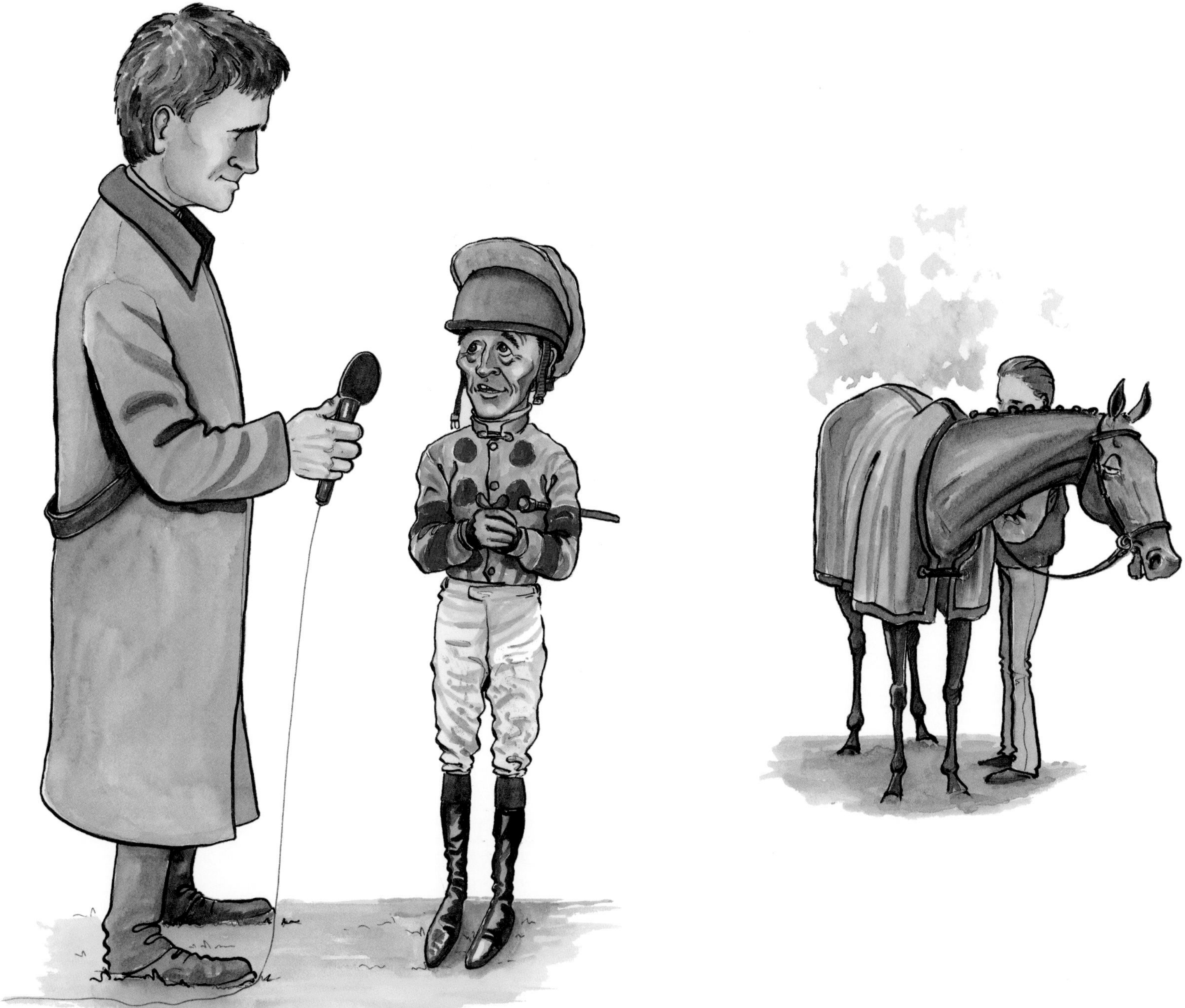

GOING...

F<small>IRM</small>...

…SOFT…

...AND **BOTTOMLESS!**

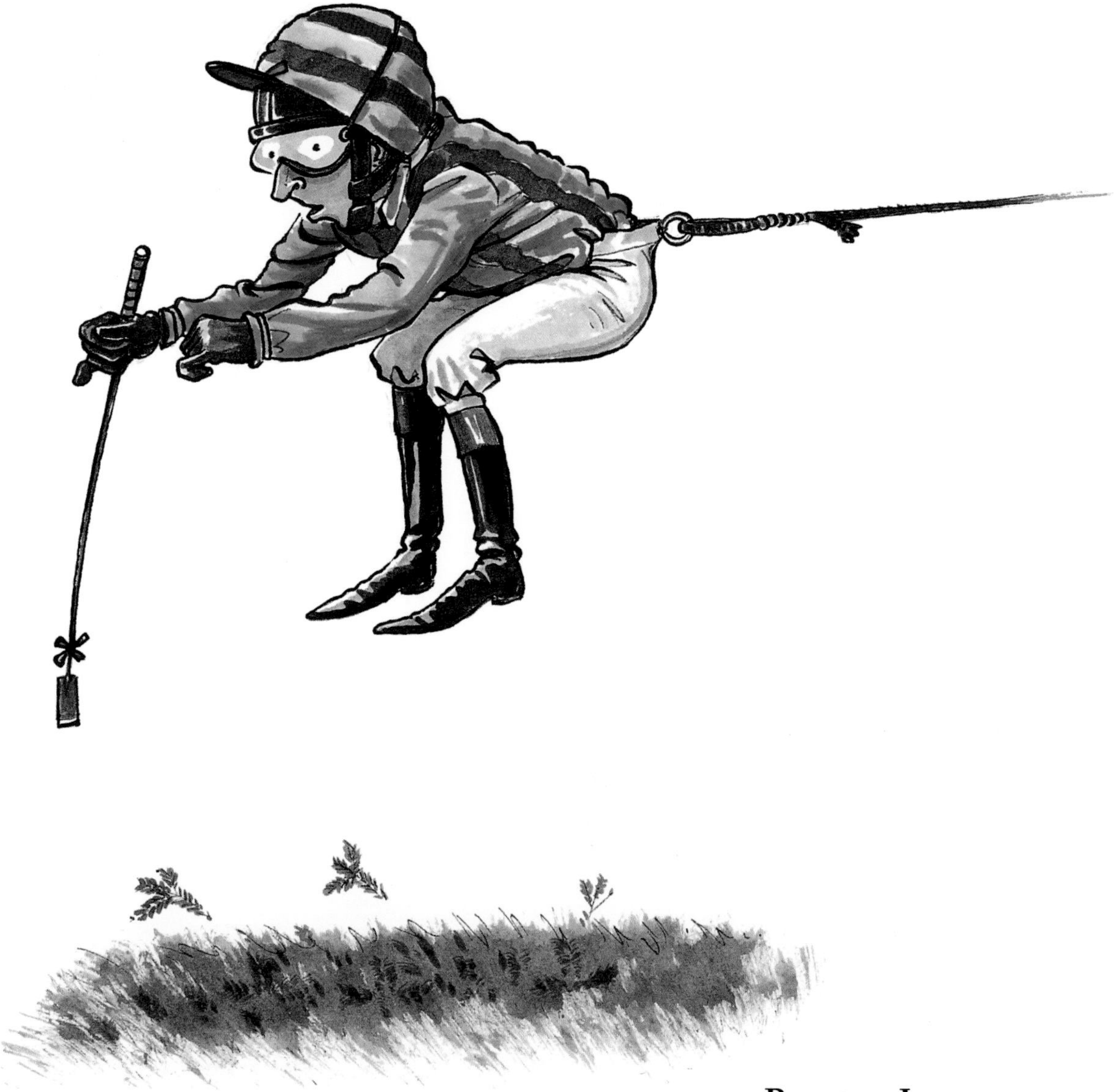

BUNGEE JUMPER

Jump Jockey...

...FLAT JOCKEY

SLIPPED DISC JOCKEY

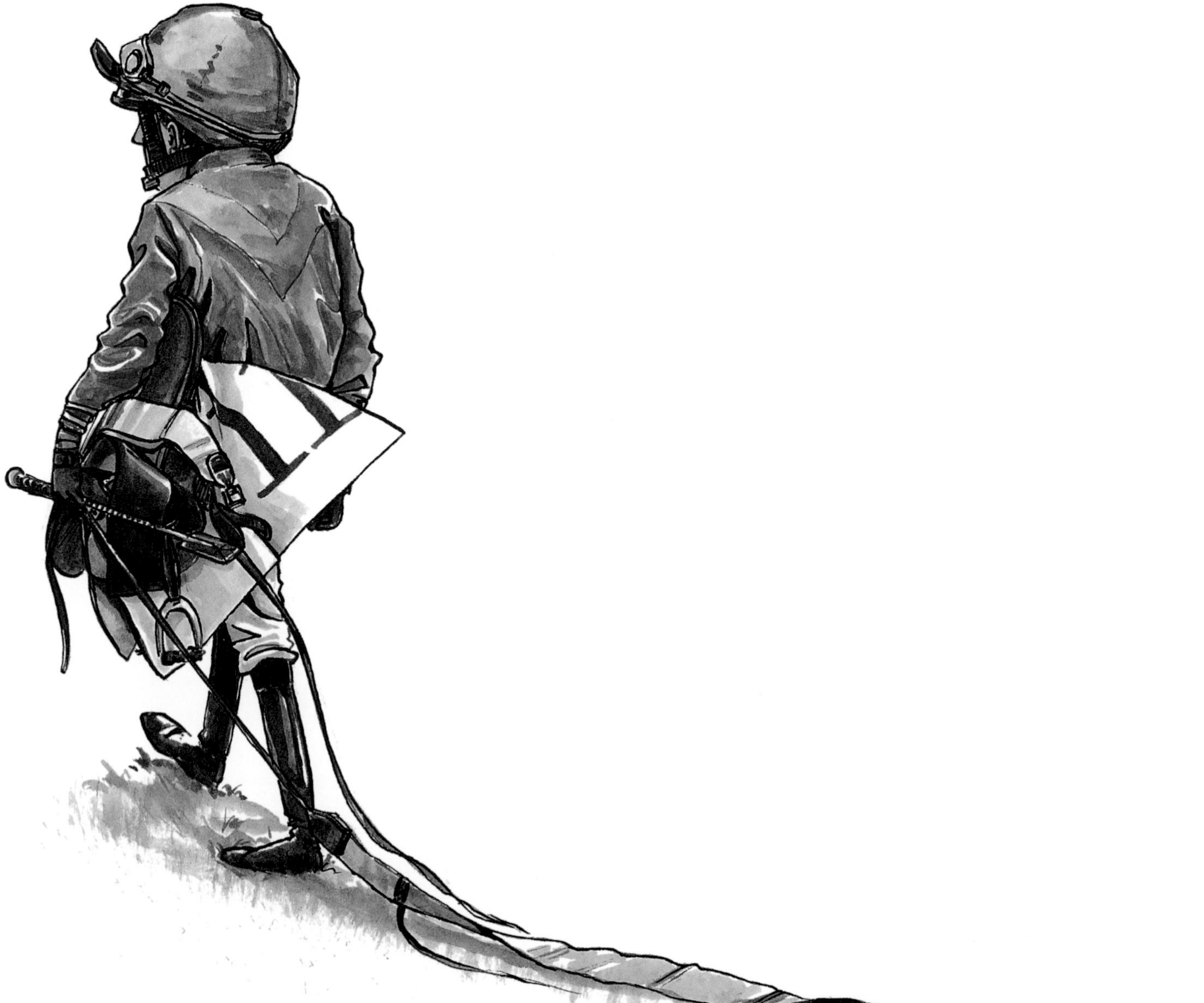

The Long Walk Home

GOING WITH THE WIND

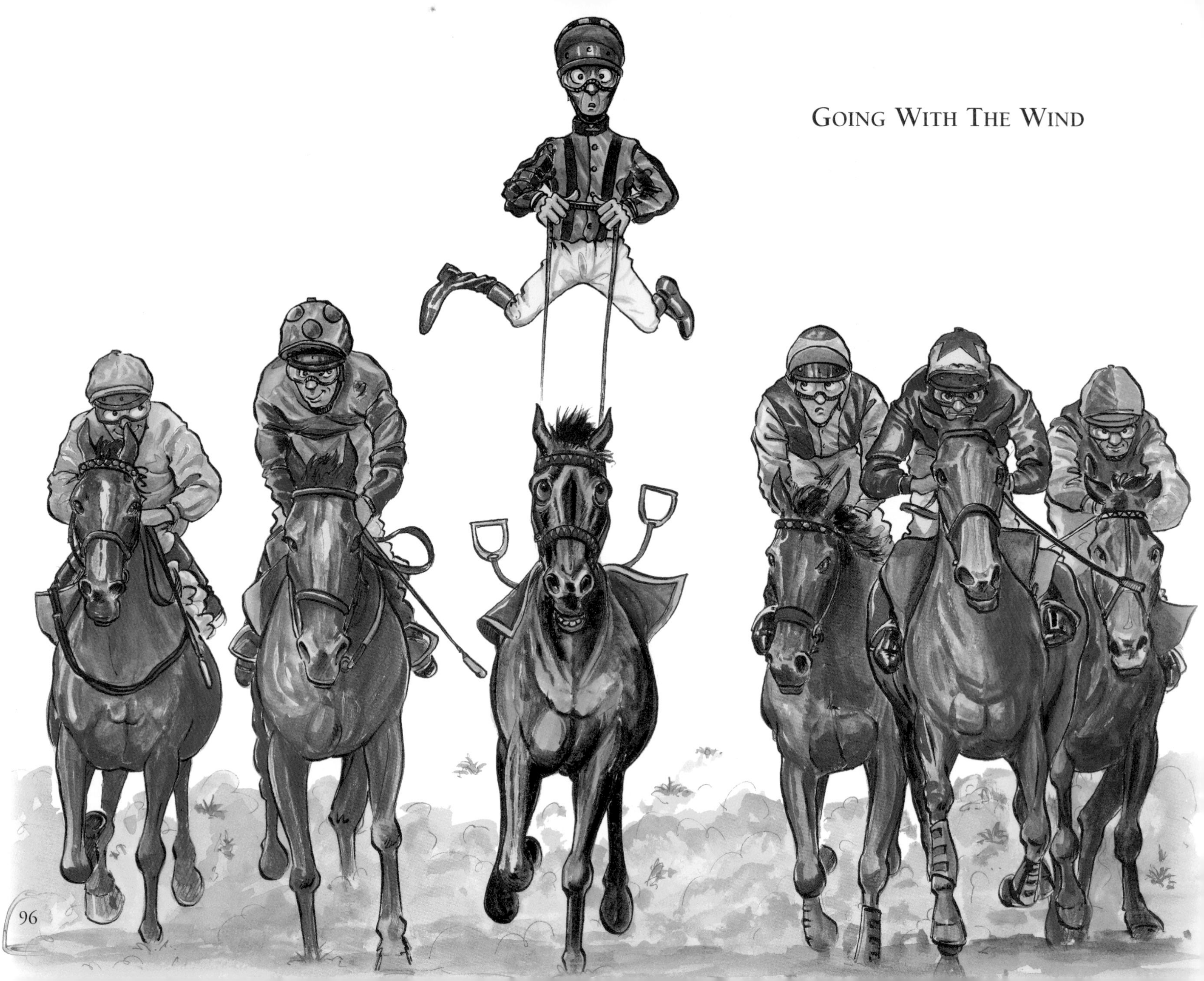

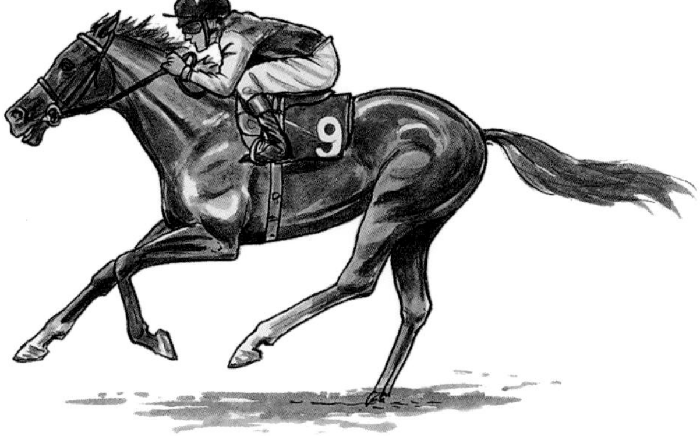
9

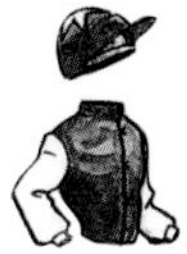

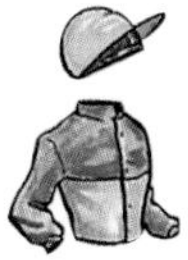

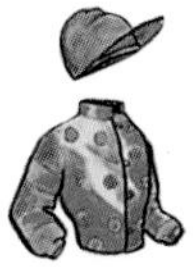

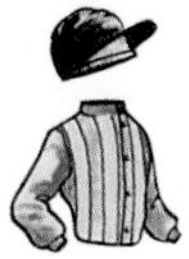

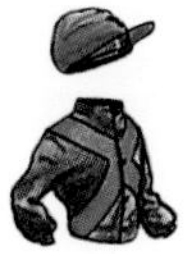

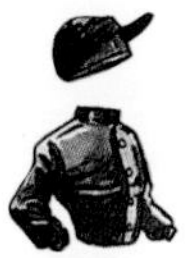

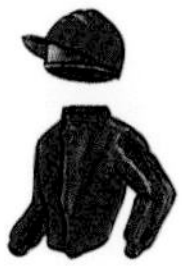

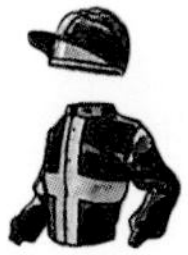

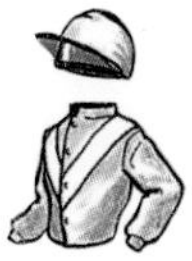

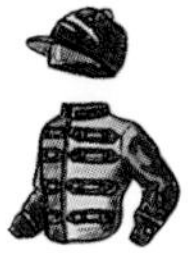

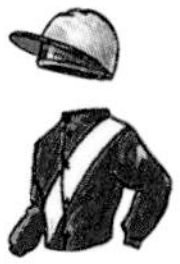

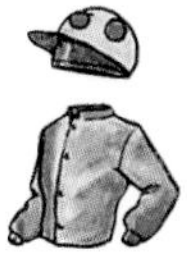

RACING…
…on the flat

SLIPPING UP

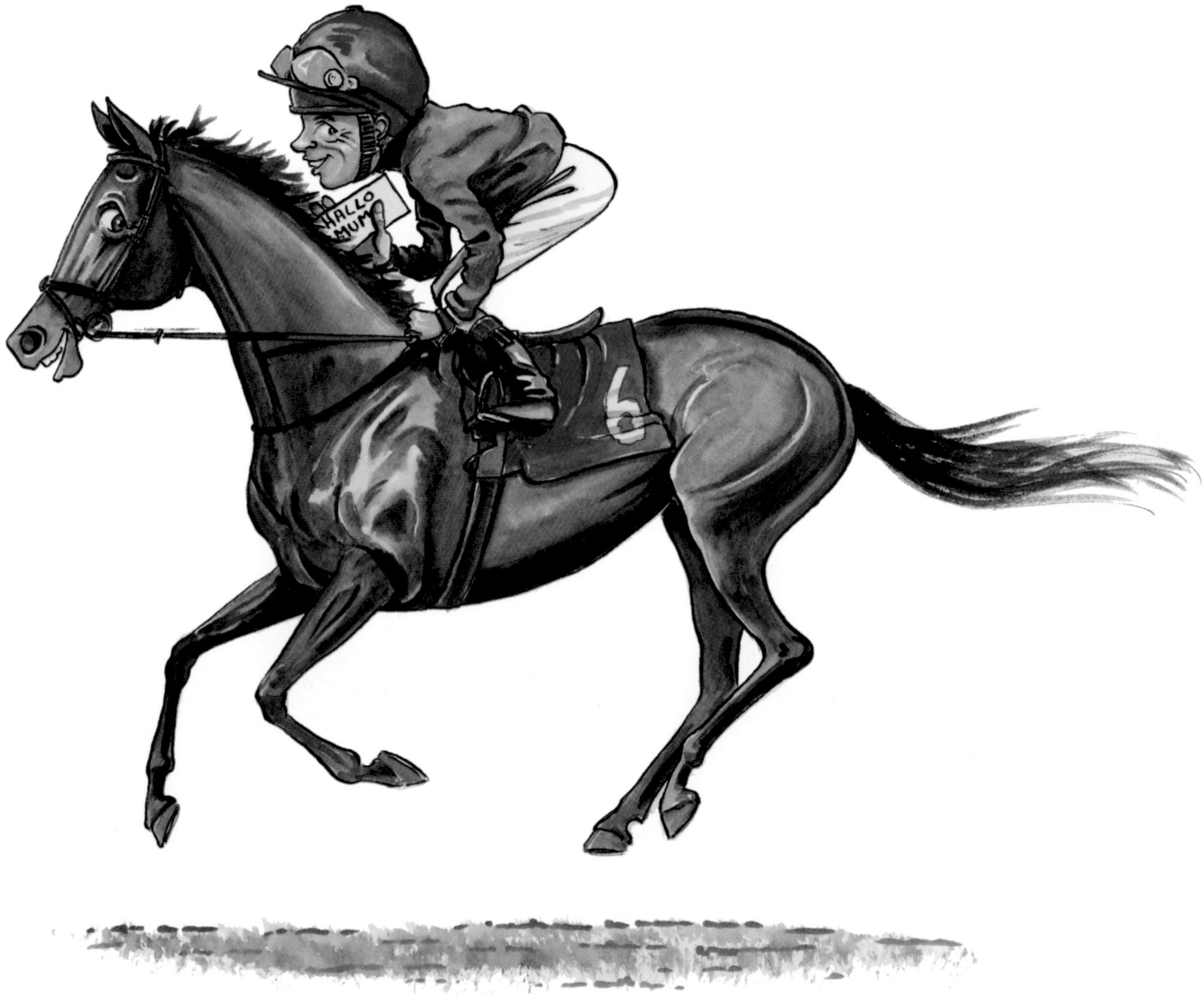
HALLO
MUM
6

Photo Finish

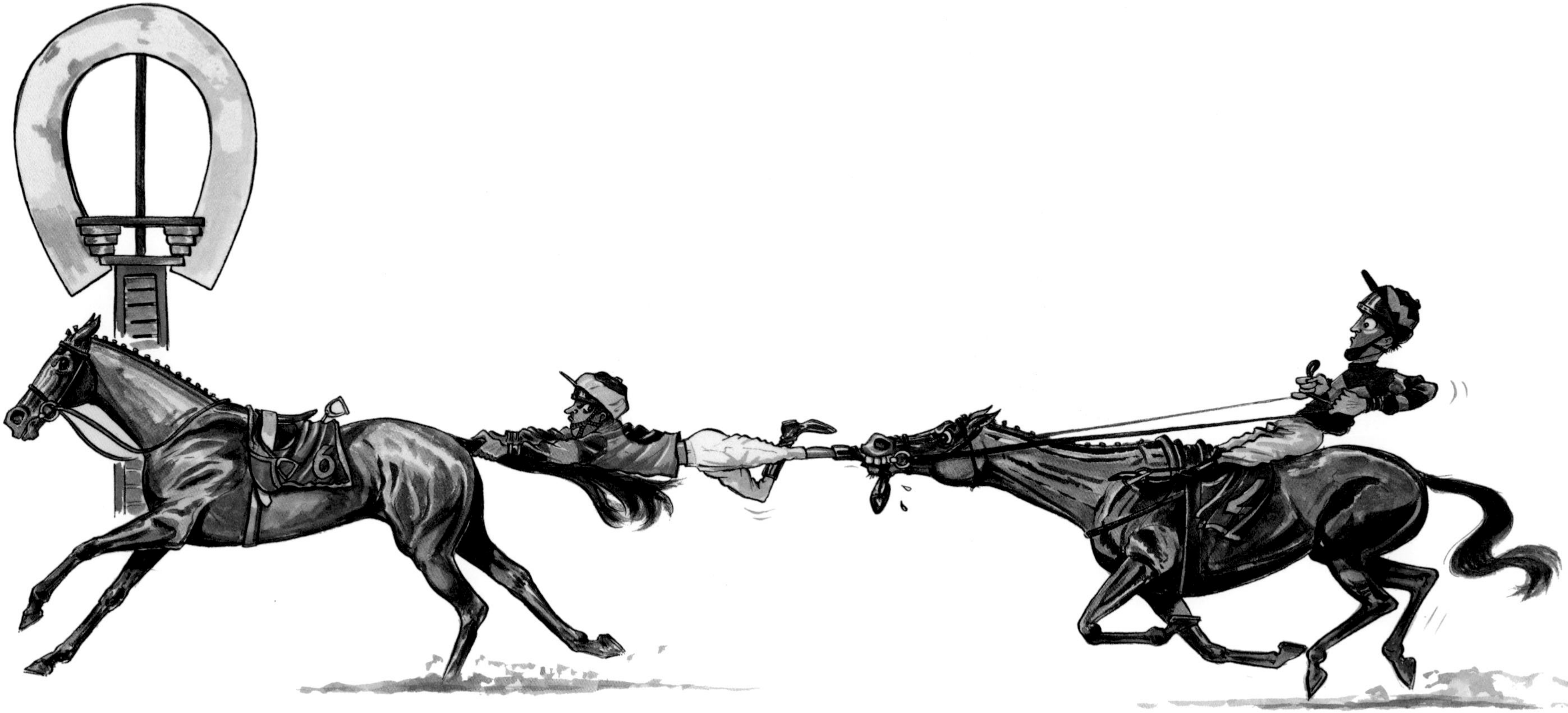

PULLING UP

USING THE WHIP

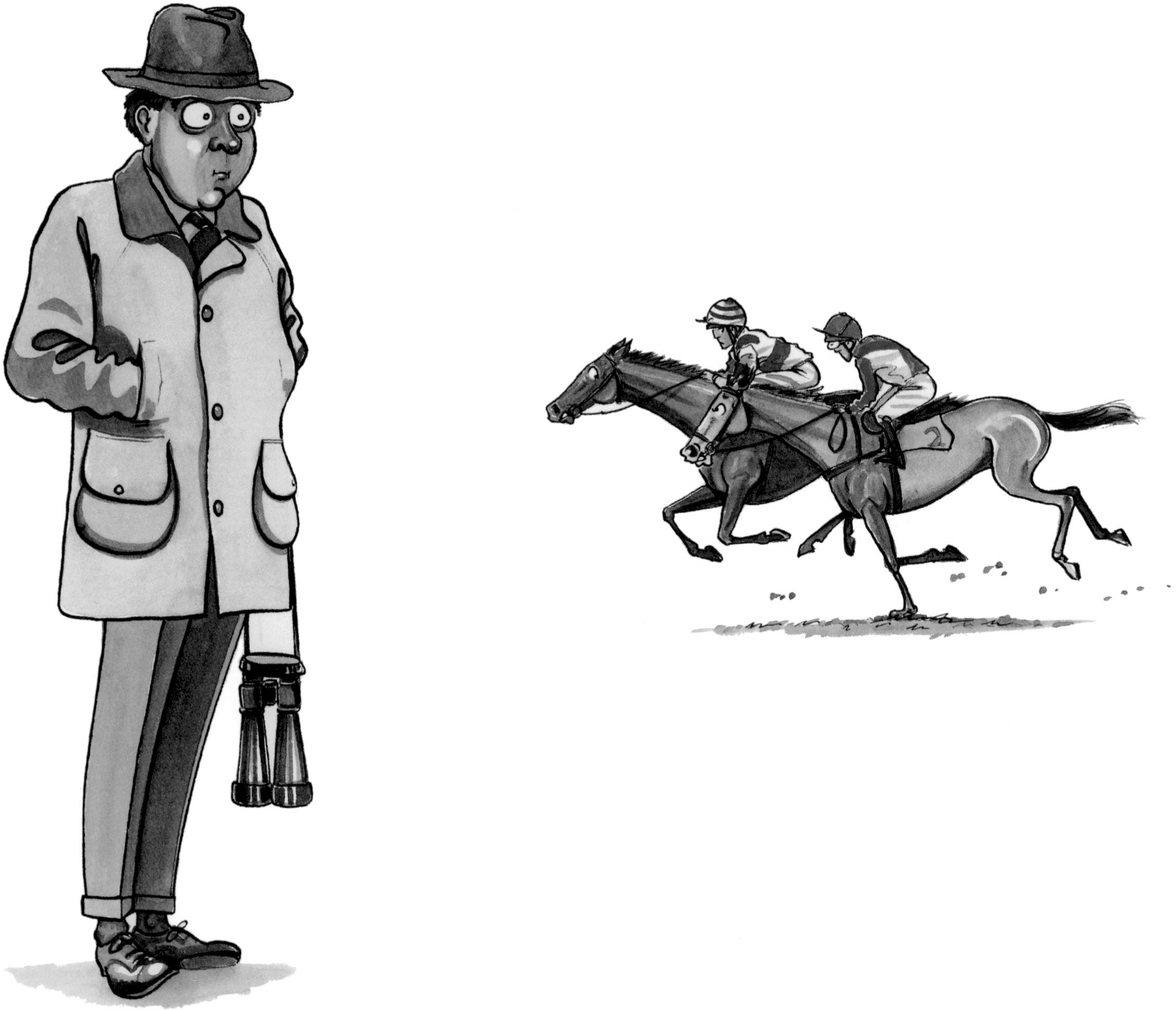

THE TRAINER

There are trainers with yards of fifty or sixty horses and lads who scurry hither and yon and raked shingle which crunches agreeably under the tyres of the owners' Bentleys and jockeys who fly in for a canter up the carefully manicured gallops and to proffer their view on whether this horse or that is ready for that big race or this. There are trainers who accompany their owners in the Gulfstream V to sales in Kentucky and never even blink as the bidding ratchets up in $100,000 clips. There are trainers who can take the long view and can see at a glance that this mare with that stallion will produce offspring which that syndicate will buy sight unseen for millions before the foal has even stood up for the first time just to make sure that another outfit cannot get its claws into the poor wee thing. And they have the names and telephone numbers in their heads and in their accounts such that the deal is no sooner said than done. Their horses are flown between continents on chartered custom Boeings wrapped in rugs that would not look out of place in a boudoir and are pampered the while by liveried lads who spend more time in the air than in the saddle. They have owners begging to

have a horse in their yards. There are waiting lists for the waiting lists. Their company is courted and their opinions solicited and their every word, nod and wink is scrutinised and analysed as if it were brought down from the mountain-top engraved on tablets of stone. They are prophets who can see potential in a yearling and alchemists who can turn base horseflesh into gold by way of Oaks, Legers, Derbys and Diamond Stakes.

Then there are the rest. Who keep three horses in the looseboxes out the back and racket from one race meeting to the next in a converted chiller lorry with a dodgy transmission. Their destinations are more often Doncaster and Sedgefield than Dubai or Chantilly; and they stay in Travelodges rather than the Four Seasons. Their gallops are a margin of grass in the winter wheat and a walker in the old cowshed replaces strings of lads. Their owners arrive not in Bentleys but in Fords and in droves at that to see their sixteenth share make the turn in front before tailing off down the run-in as half the field pass him in the last few

furlongs. Their jockeys don't fly in for a race here and there. They live locally and take what rides they can get, do what they can with a horse and dream of the last minute call that will whisk them to Cheltenham or Ascot and glory.

And their horses are triers and stayers but very seldom winners; and they know that if ever an Arkle, or a Tetrarch or a Shergar or a Seabiscuit were ever to be decanted from a lorry into their laps the chances are that shortly after that first astonishing, glorious, triumphant and luck affirming outing where the newcomer romps home at long odds by any number of lengths, the owners would find themselves under siege from the big boys and enfiladed from all side with promises of trophies, fame and fortune if only the horse were just in the right hands. Step this way.

One thing remains the same however on either side of the great divide. For jockeys, trainers and owners alike, and it makes no odds whether it is a classic or the local meeting handicap stakes, the first five minutes after your horse sails first past the post is a glimpse of heaven. It's why they do it.

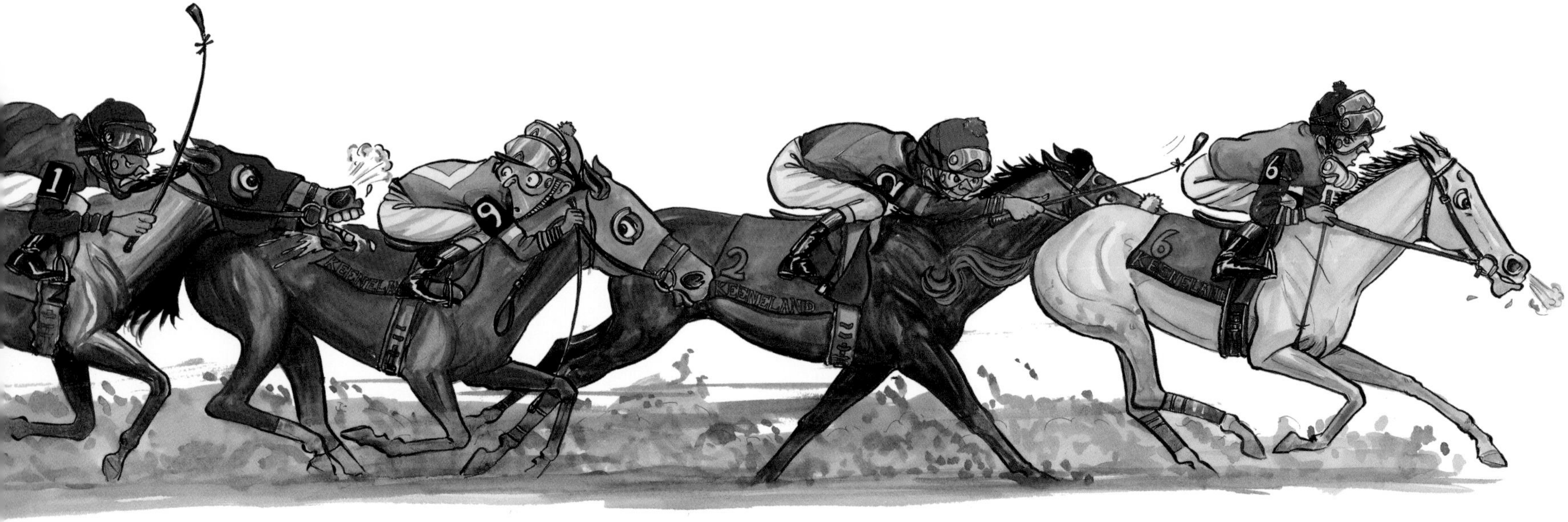
KEENELAND

The American Way

POLO

105

FORE!

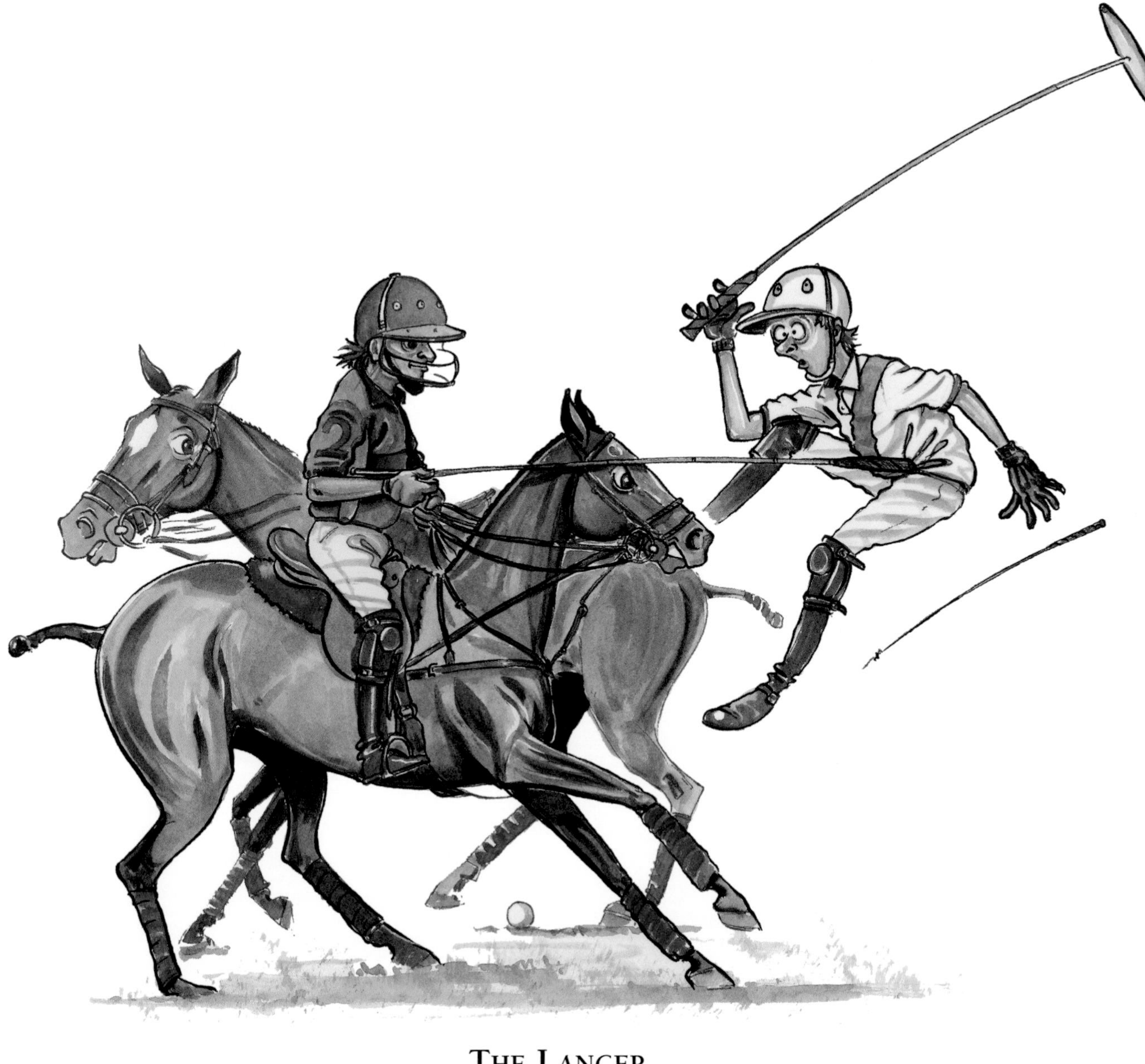

The Lancer

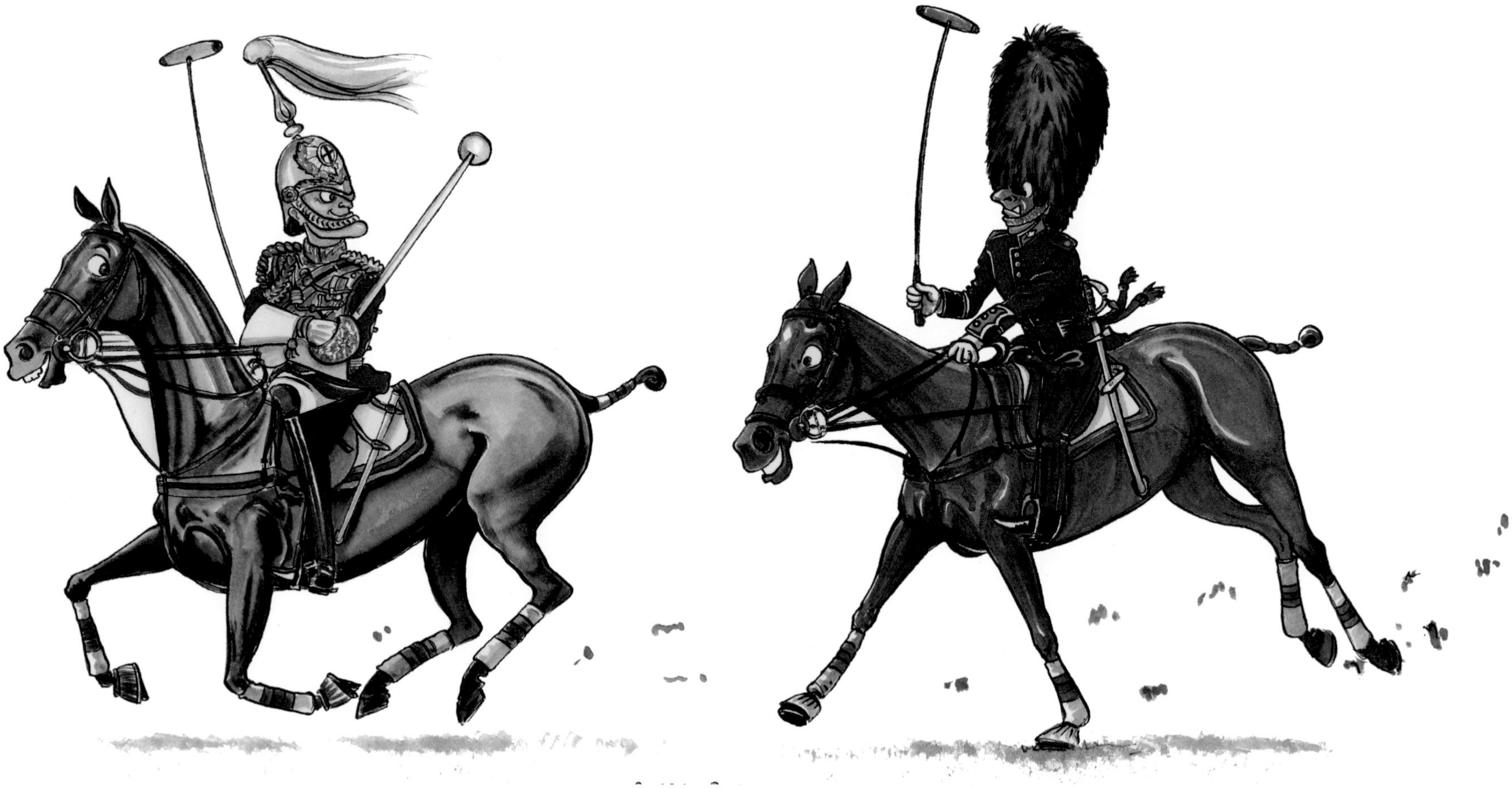

Guards Polo

DEFENCE CUTS

CAUGHT BEHIND

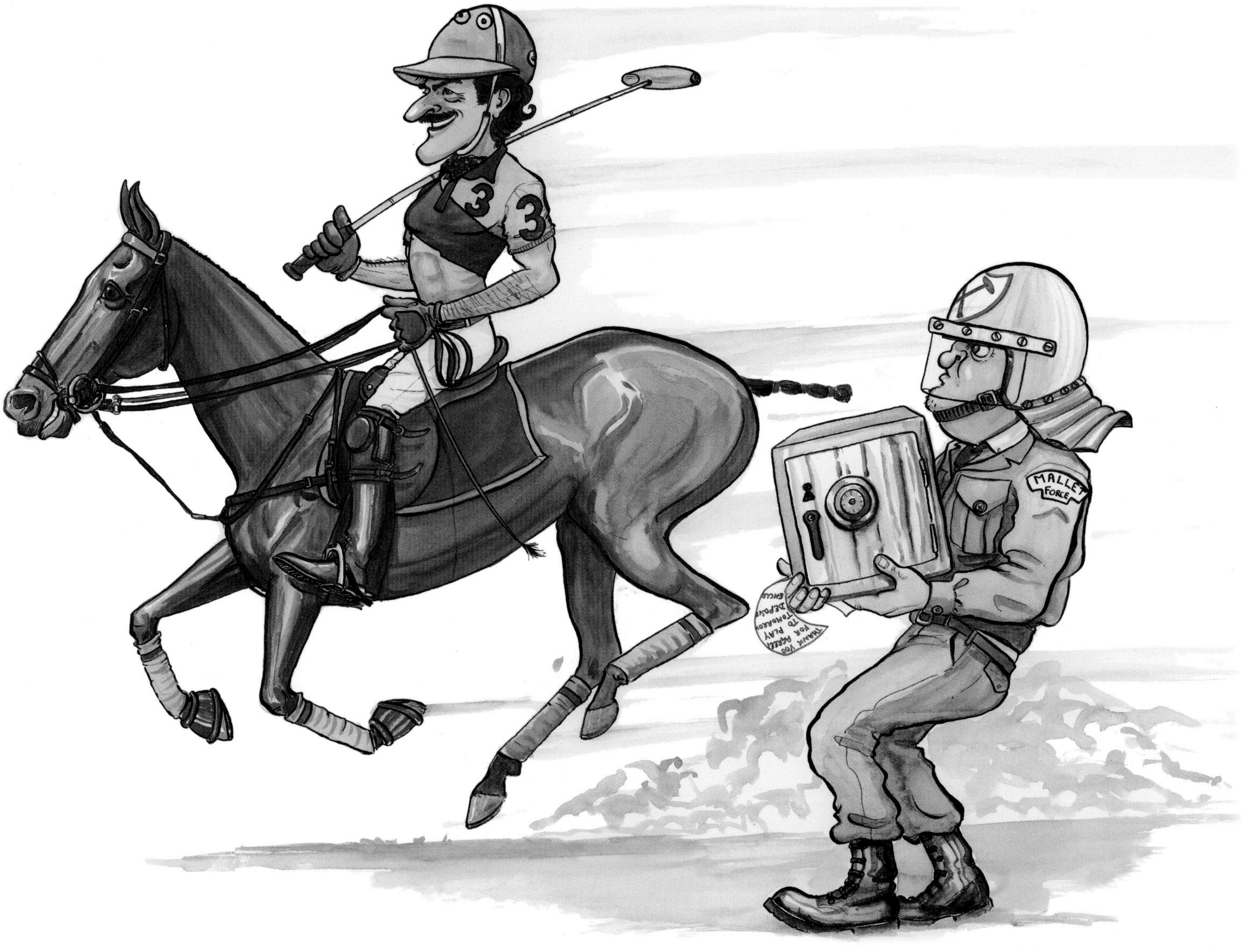
3
3
THANK YOU
FOR AGREE
PLAY
TO TOMORROW
DEPOSIT
ENCL
MALLET
FORCE

THE PROFESSIONAL'S FEE

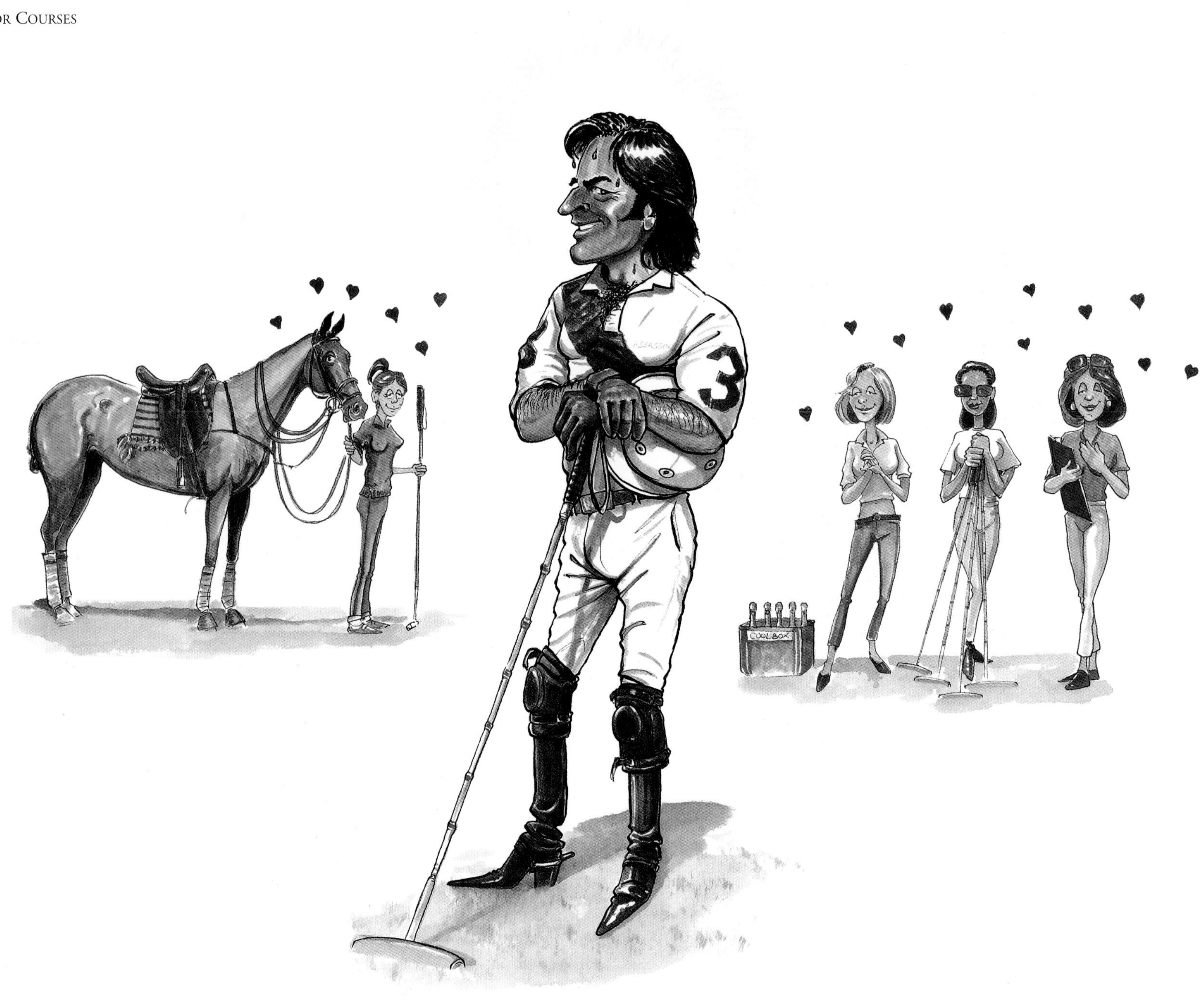
3
COOLBOX

THE ASSASSIN

Enrique is the last word in polo chic. Which is to say that he is a fully paid up South American high goal assassin. He could ride before he could walk and was roping cattle with the gauchos on Daddy's estancha not long after that. Indeed it was during an early altercation with a recalcitrant longhorn that he acquired the long and puckered scar down his ribs that causes such a frisson of wicked contemplation among the sillier sort of female spectator when Enrique is slipping into a fresh shirt between chukkas. Naturally Enrique took to the game as the proverbial mallardo takes to agua and by the time he had been drummed out of half a dozen schools at home for bunking off to ride and to play he was already making a modest reputation among the cognoscenti. He was picked up by a spotter for one of the big US high goal teams who was cruising the grounds in Rio looking for ponies and players and soon found himself as first reserve for one of the Kentucky blue chip teams. By the time he was twenty Enrique was a ten goal handicap and launched on the high goal circuit in earnest.

Which means $2,000 a week and the use of a Mercedes sports car just for openers. He requires a dozen ponies and the services of three grooms to keep them in shape. He also needs a personal trainer and a masseuse to be available around the clock in case any part of him needs loosening off after a particularly strenuous day. Or night. Since in accordance with tradition the raven haired, sparkly eyed, rug chested and deliriously sweaty high goaler Enrique devotes much of his time to running amok among the prettiest and most vacuous of the polo poppets who wilt before his dazzling smile and subside into passenger seat, his arms and, later, his bed with a sigh of admiration at the size of his mallet. Time was when Enrique had to be content with cutting a dash among the grooms, but now that he is a top caballero on the high goal merry-go-round the daughters of the international super rich are his chosen prey unless he opts for experience over mere stamina and chases their mothers instead. Play polo, make love, take the money, move on – this is Enriqe's mantra as he swans between the United States and Europe and on to Australia and the Asian season beyond.

Of course, he is very good. During a match he seems to be welded to the stirrups though he has been known to plunge dramatically into the turf in front of the grandstand if something especially blonde and pneumatic and rich catches his eye enough to want to make an early impression. He rides his horses into the ground but then they aren't his and he's there to score goals not to run some kind of equine rest home. At the end of the match he scarcely breaks step as he throws his reins to one groom, his gear to another and slides into the Mercedes next to the popsy elect of the day and guns it for the nearest champagne bar followed by restaurant followed by nightclub and away for a quick charge at the posts on the polo pitch of passion and away to the next venue before the sun has dried the dew on the lawns. Where his grooms will be waiting with new jeans and shirts, polished boots, fresh horses ready to start the new day. One day Enrique will retire from being an international high goal assassin and go back to roping cattle. In the meantime he has a new contract for a series of matches in Brunei. Poor lamb. *Vaya con dios!*

THE PATRON

'Tell them I'm offering to take a million shares at five bucks per and if they don't come back within the hour the price comes down. By the weekend those numbers will be burning a hole in their little brains you could drive a truck through. And tell them I'll take the lease on their HQ into the bargain. We can level it later and extend the car park. Screw the listing. Accidents happen. Call me when it's sorted.'

'Yessir! Nossir! Three bags full, Sir!'

The patron emerges from his office in the rear of the twelve berth Mercedes trailer well satisfied with the way things are going and calls for his boots and another shirt. He pauses briefly to caress the velvety muzzle of one of the ponies as he moves along the corridor. 'There, sweetheart,' he murmurs, 'who's gonna be papa's top pony this afternoon then? 'Course you are, aren't you? 'Cos papa doesn't want to call the cannery, does papa? No, he doesn't, does he?' And moves on. Polo has much to offer.

The patron has jetted in on the Gulfstream and choppered down for two days of intensive R&R in the saddle. Polo advances his interests and supplies his needs on many levels. It's good exercise, of course, and though his physicians have told him that careering around on horseback at full tilt and plummeting betimes headfirst into the sod is not altogether what they had in mind when they advised a modest fitness regime in his relentless schedule, his commitment to vigorous sport actually reduces the life insurance premiums as long as the sawbones don't blab to the underwriters the exact nature of his hobby. So that's a win on all fronts. Polo has much to offer.

Then there is the chance to mingle with the great and the good who can only add to the extensive collection of silver framed photos on the Steinway baby grands which decorate the morning rooms of his various houses from Melbourne to Malibu and back again via London, New York, Monaco and Milan. Of course, he has to show off outrageously at the charity auctions which inevitably follow lunch in the marquee but then what else is money for when you come down to it? It's all tax deductible in one or other of the jurisdictions where he and his sprawling commercial empire are resident for the time being according to the availability of investment inducements, tax breaks and subsidies and what's a hundred grand going to get you these days? The ponies and the gaucho high goal assassins and the grooms and the drivers and the pilots eat that sort of petty cash in a week. But none of his business contacts is going to turn down his invitations to social events of this magnitude and any number of doors may open and opportunities present themselves as the result. Not least from amongst the winding tail of long-limbed and coltish lovelies who populate the polo grounds around the world like so many rare and fragrant orchids just waiting to be plucked to decorate the patron's arm at the championship ball and who knows what and where beyond while Madame patron remains safely in Milan or Monaco or Melbourne or Malibu via New York or London. Polo has much indeed to offer.

And he buys his ponies like his shirts; by the dozen, matching and with his initials on. And when they have been stretched beyond repair by his six foot plus, fifteen stone easy, bulk he passes them, like his shirts, down the line to others with a magnanimous wave. They may have names to their grooms but to the patron they are just another asset. Like the jet or the chopper or the twelve berth Mercedes trailer or the high goal assassins who advance his interests and provide his needs as he emerges from his office calling for his boots and another shirt. 'And make sure they're good and stained this time, for Chrissakes, I don't want to look like a pansy amateur in the semi final! And get Tokyo on the sat-phone by the end of the chukka. I don't care. Wake the buggers up!'

'Yessir! Nossir! Three bags full, sir!'

The patron ignores the wave of a minor European royal as he pulls on his boots.

Polo has much to offer.

FULL STRETCH

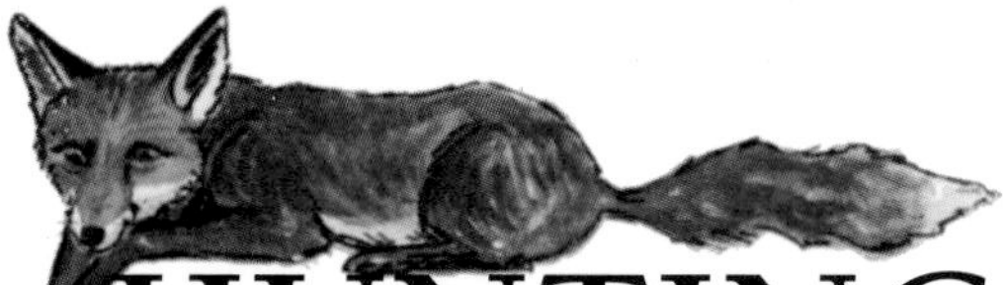

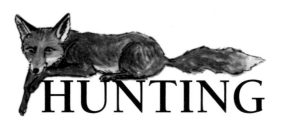

HUNTING

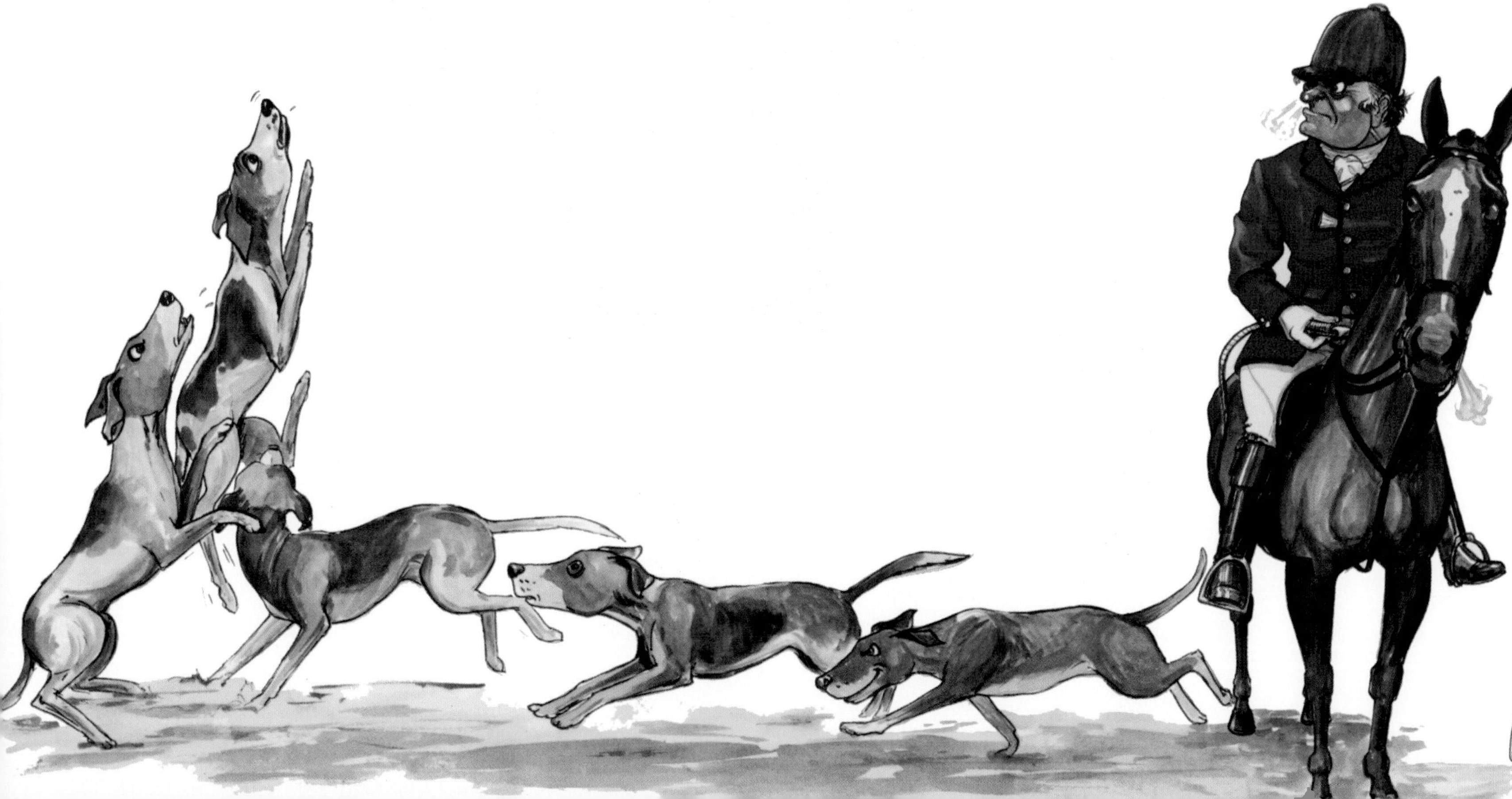

THE JOINT MASTER

Patricia is small and round and dark and dangerous. Patricia is the joint master. Patricia is scary. Patricia is not scary because she is joint master; Patricia is joint master because she is scary. Patricia is married to Simon. It is widely thought that Simon married Patricia because he didn't dare not to. Patricia's father wasn't sure that he wanted Patricia to marry Simon because he didn't think that Simon deserved Patricia. He didn't think that anyone deserved Patricia because she was so scary, but he couldn't save Simon in the end because he wouldn't face Patricia.

Patricia's mother was joint master too. She was pretty scary, but nothing like as scary as Patricia. So when her mother retired as joint master – she was well over seventy and still hunting twice a week – there was a bit of a debate and a quick vote and then they made Patricia joint master. And a very good joint master she is too. Committee meetings are brief, concise and to the point. Patricia tends to chair them and when Patricia's hand goes up, everyone else's hands go up

too. When Patricia's hand stays down it would be a brave man or woman to raise theirs. The committee is not renowned for its bravery. Her mother saw to that.

They don't let her anywhere near the farmers, that would not be politic at all, but when it comes to rounding up the subscriptions or selling tickets for the hunt ball or pulling in the sponsorship for the point-to-point Patricia is something to see in action. Then her scariness comes in rather handy. Slightly like a fire ship among the Spanish fleet. Small but likely to go off at any moment.

And as field master she is happy to lead from the front, sailing through hedges like a small round tank and ploughing across ditches rather as a landing craft addresses the beachhead. Sustained by long draughts from her saddle flask which is reputed to contain fifty/fifty schnapps and gin, no one can keep up with her. The ladies prefer to canter round the field margins looking for the gate or the bridge; the juniors don't have the legs for it and the men, frankly, don't have

the nerve. The oldest member, resplendent in his rat-catcher, drew abreast of her once as they were careering along the valley bottom beside the river on a racketing six mile point with the hounds in full cry and going like billy be damned and you'd think from the noise there'd been murder done. Patricia never let up for a moment but gave him such a dressing down before showing him the second best view in England that the old boy had to pull up to catch his breath. He was reportedly found later leaning against a tree muttering 'Just like her mother in the air raids, damn it!' Scary.

TOP HAT...   ...FLAT HAT

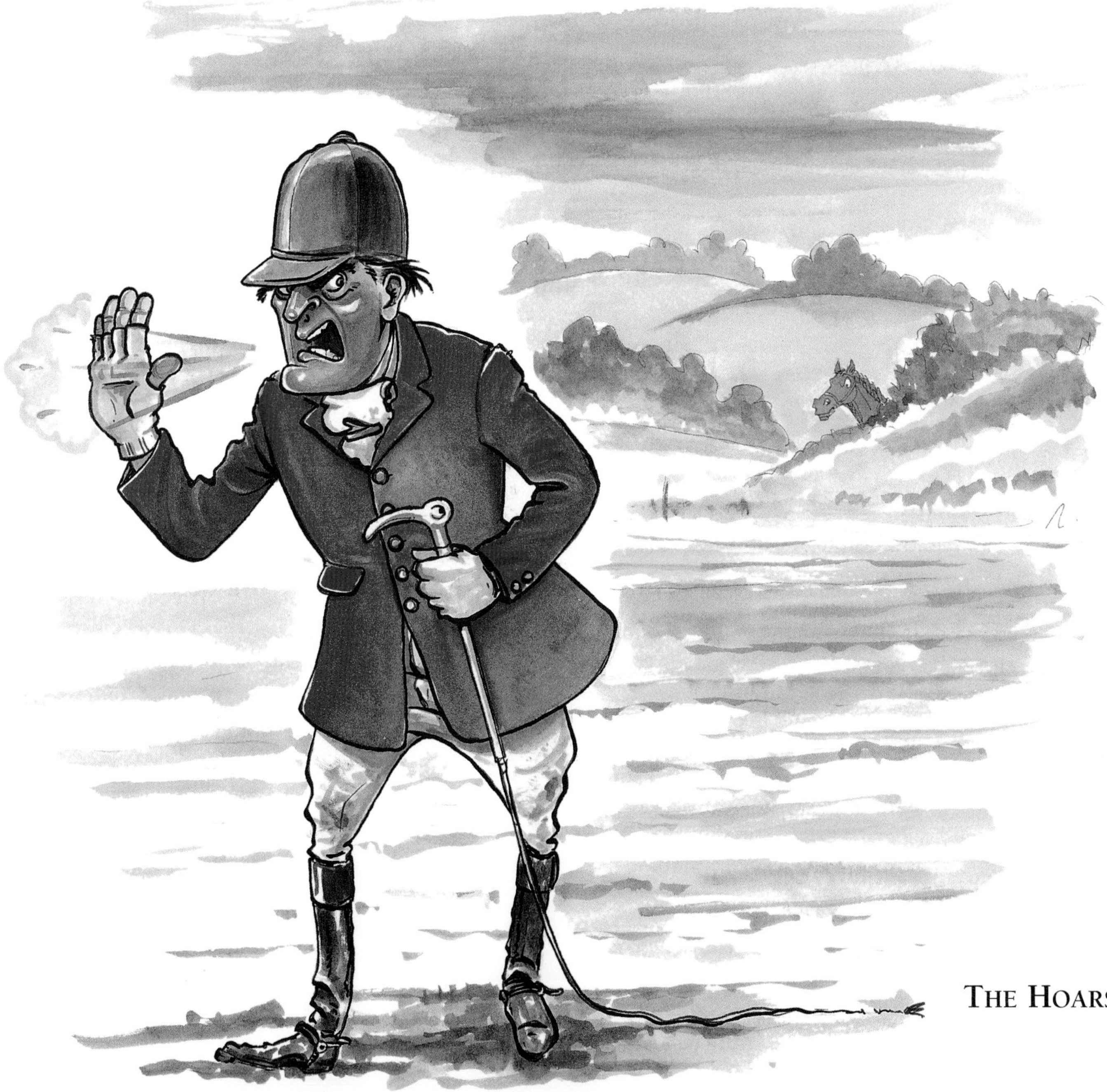

The Hoarse Whisperer

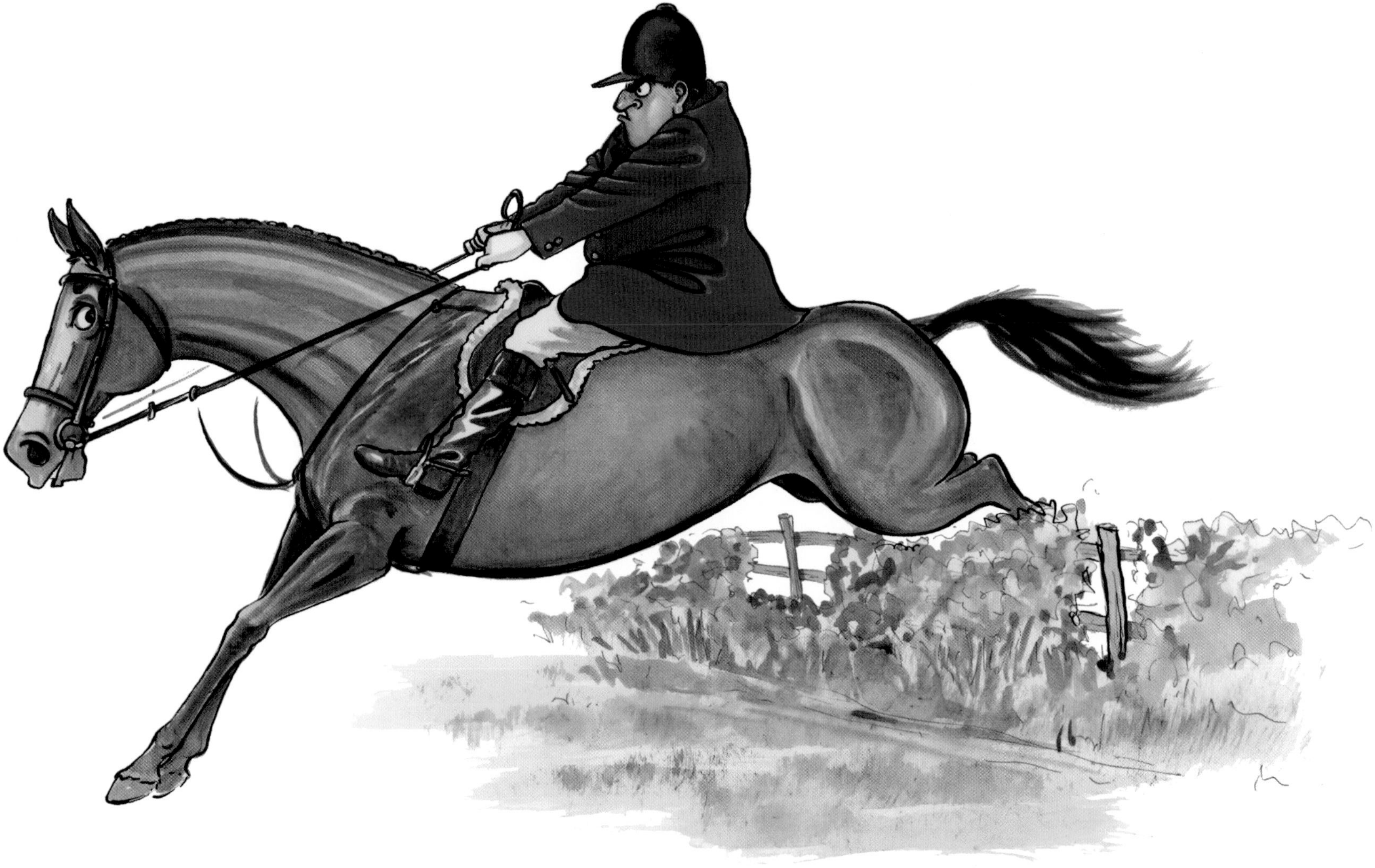

THE BACK SEAT DRIVER

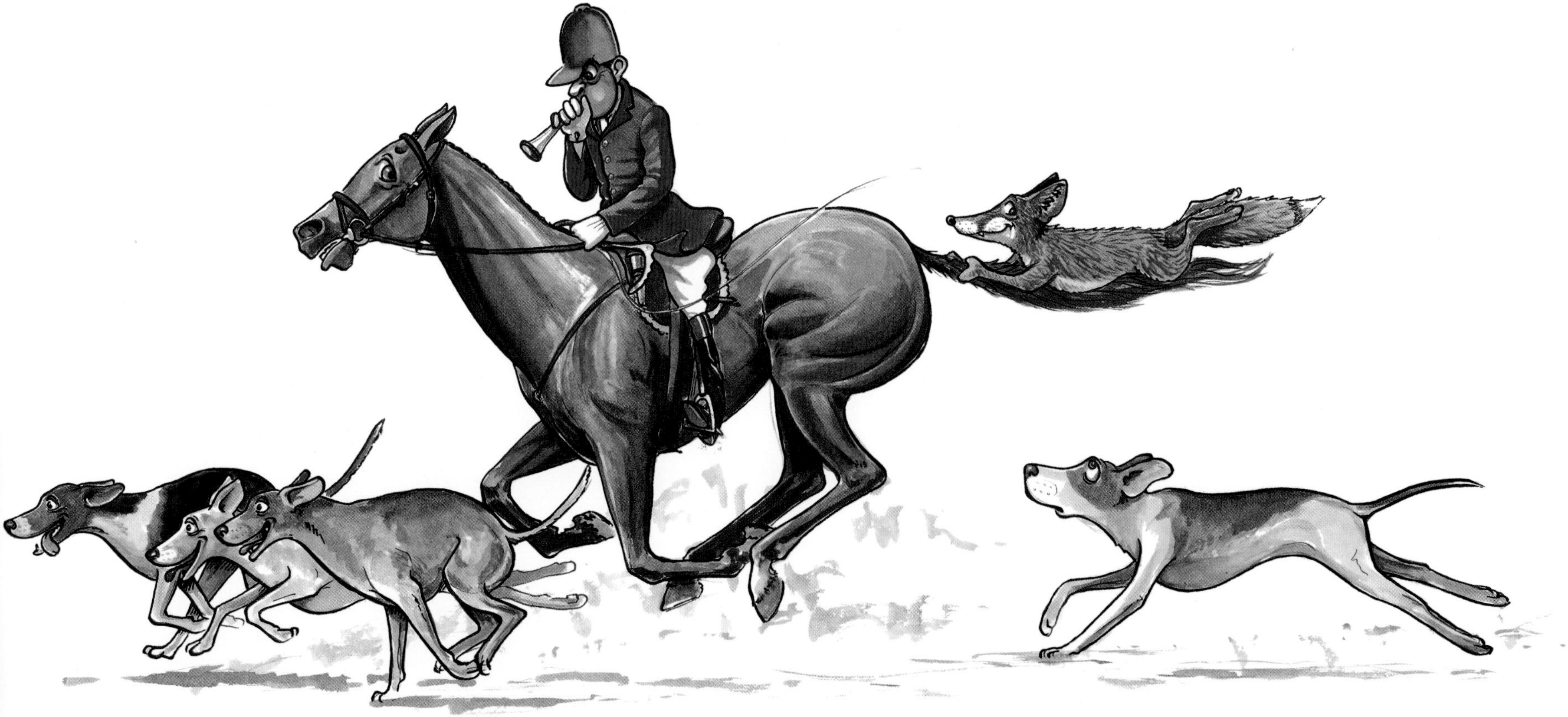

TAIL END CHARLIE

THE HUNTING DAY

PREPARATION

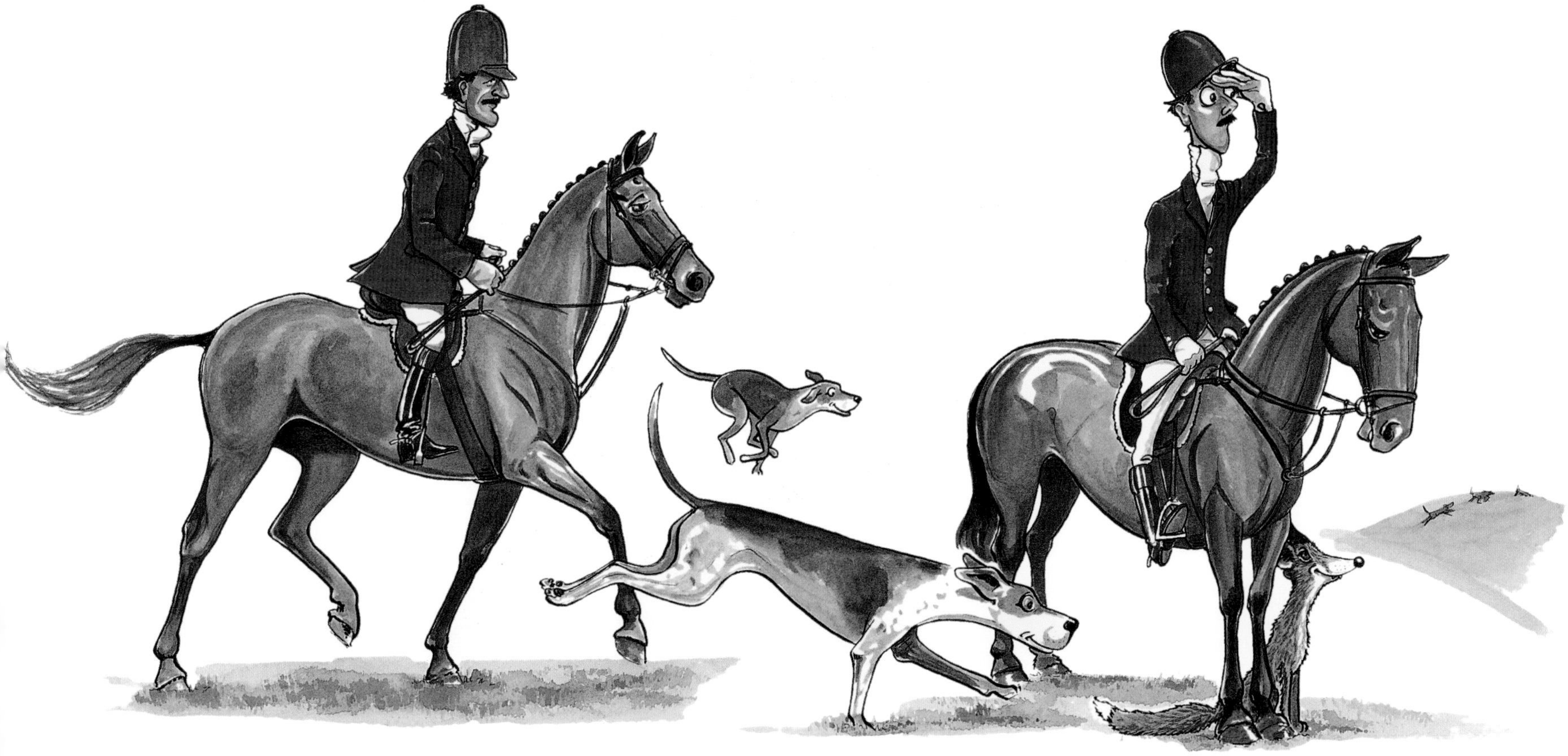

Anticipation

Exploration

DEFORESTATION

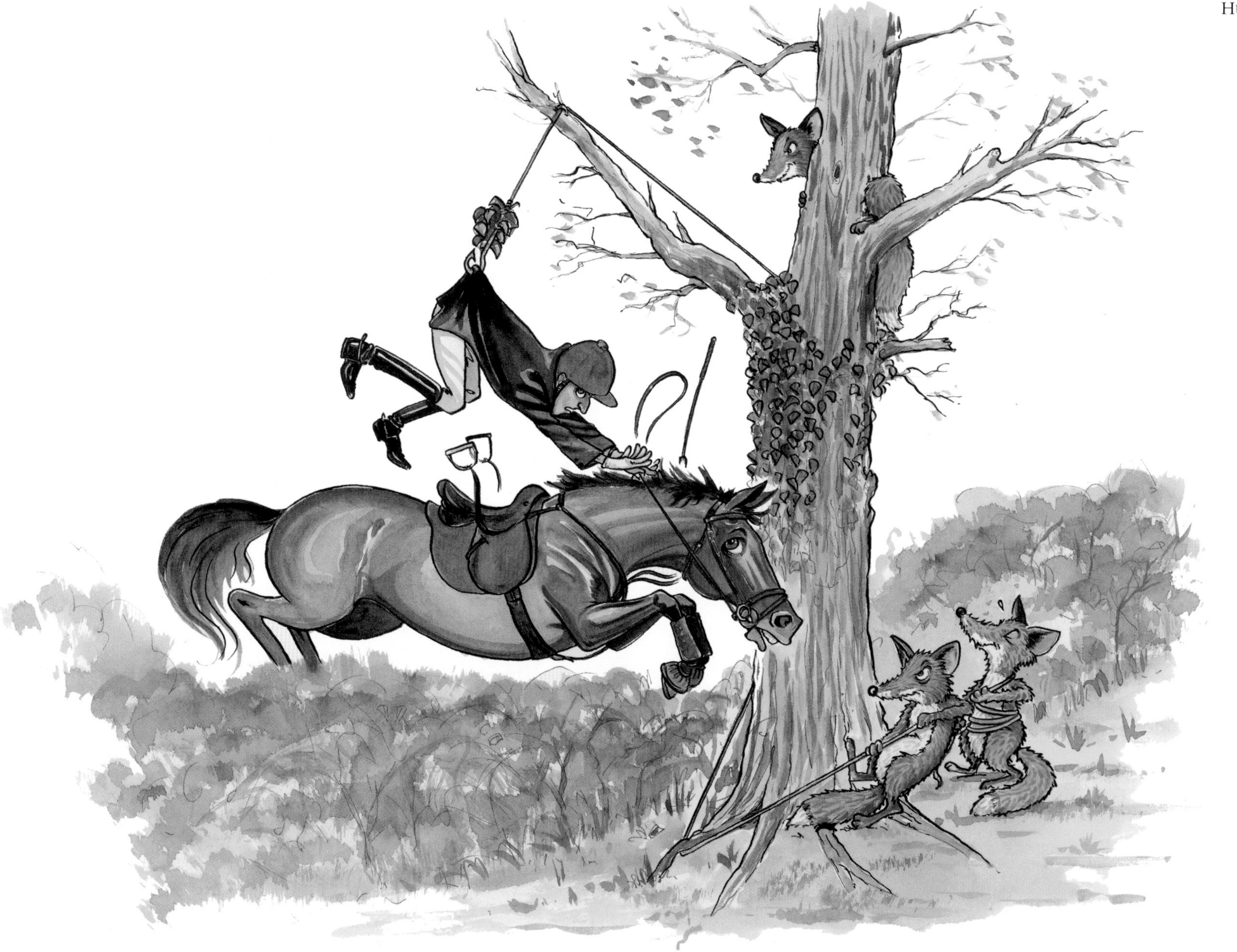

Out Foxed

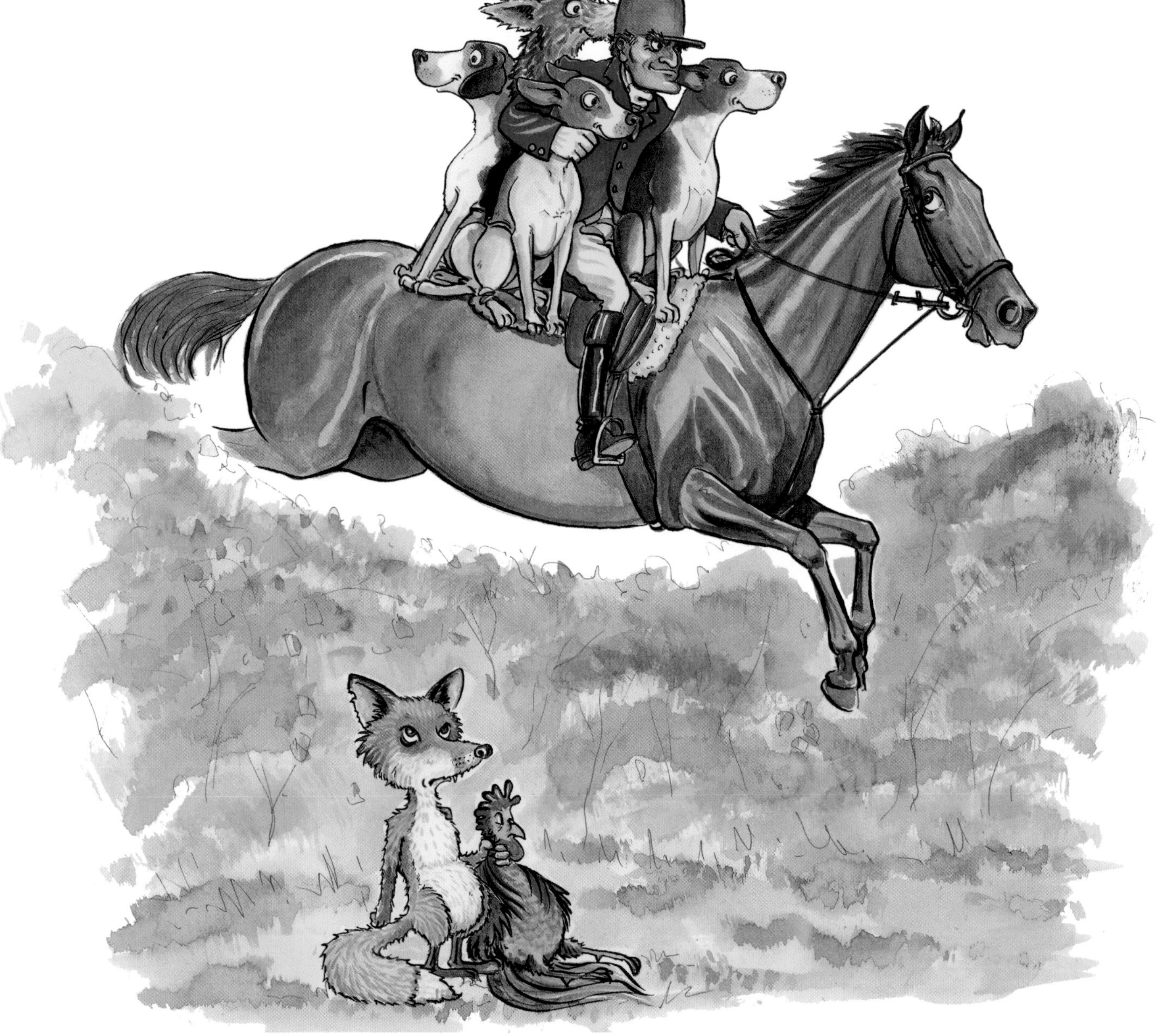

The Flying Squad

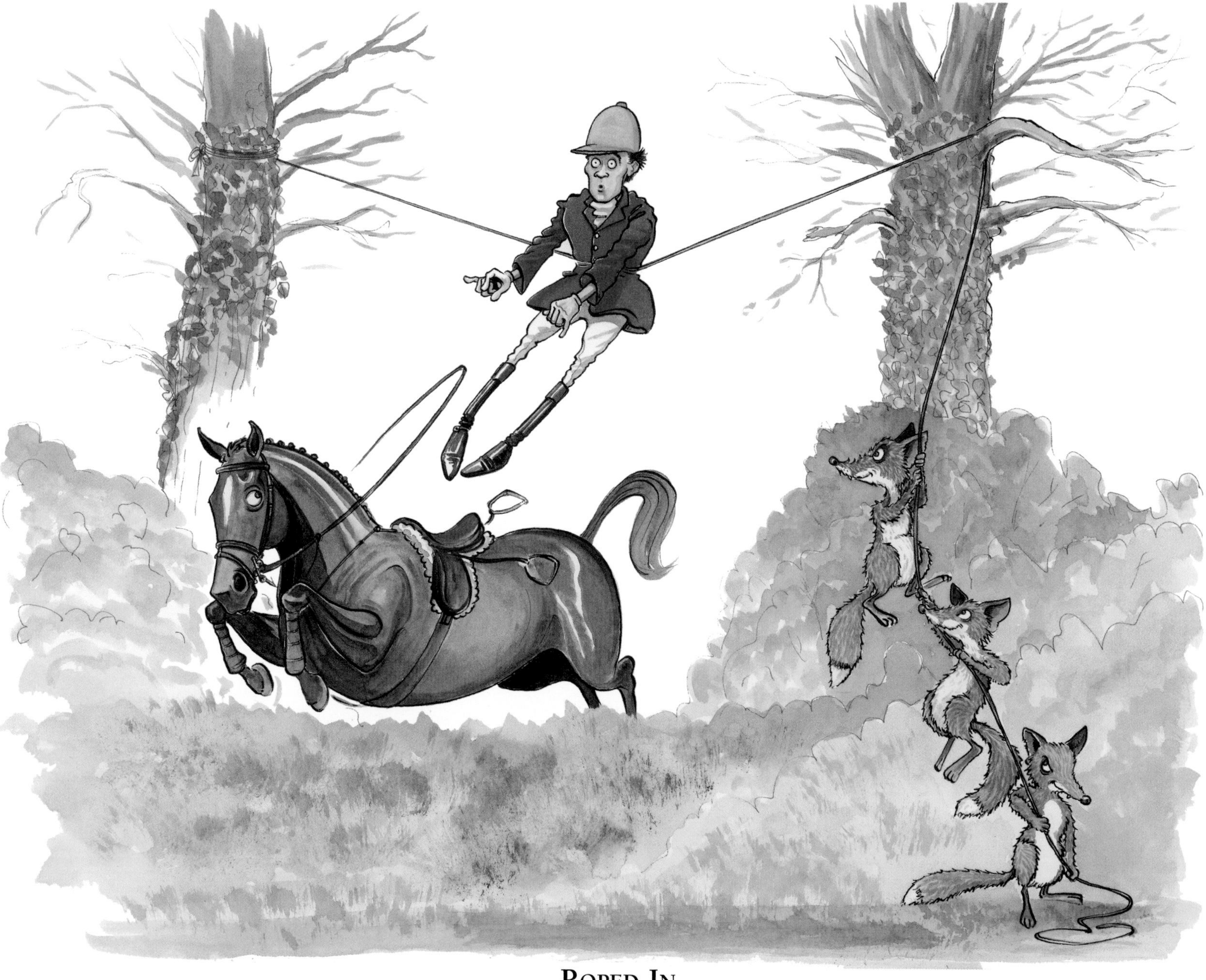

Roped In

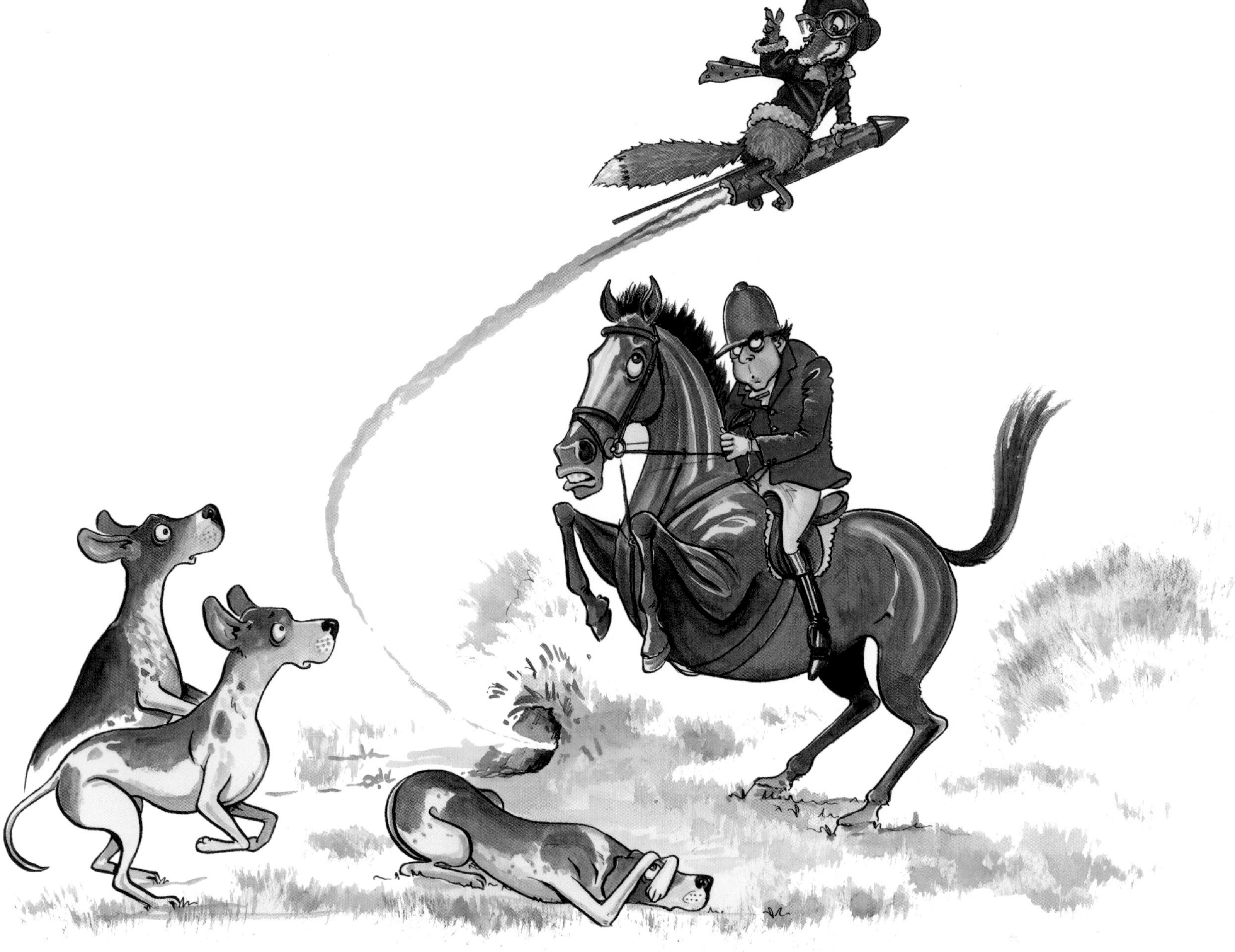

Flying Fox

21ST CENTURY FOX

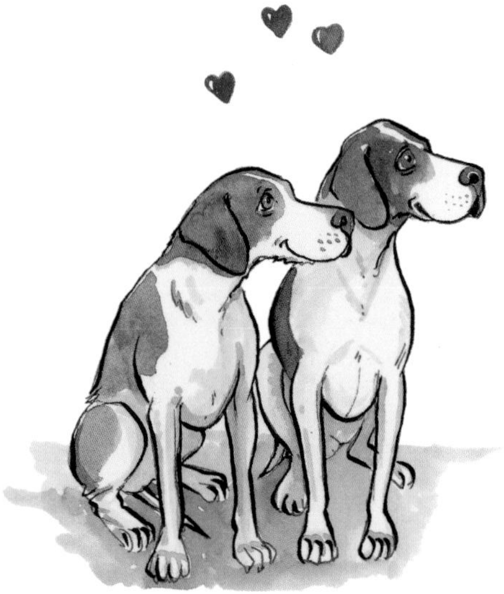

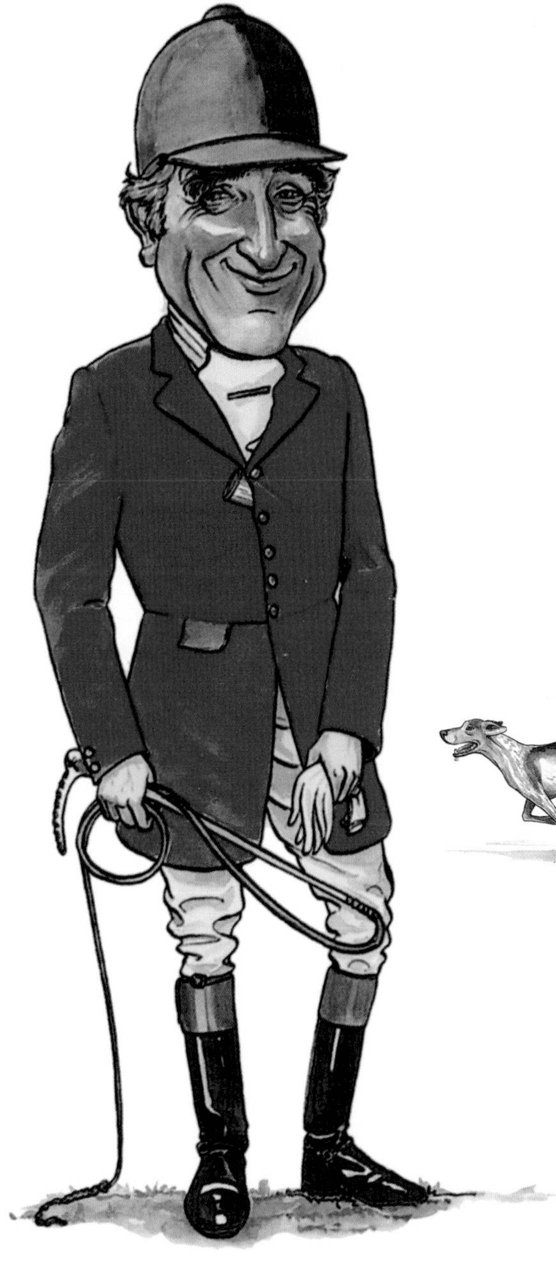

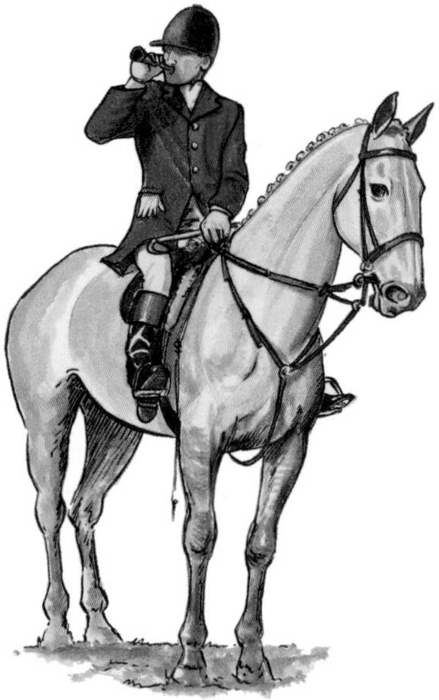

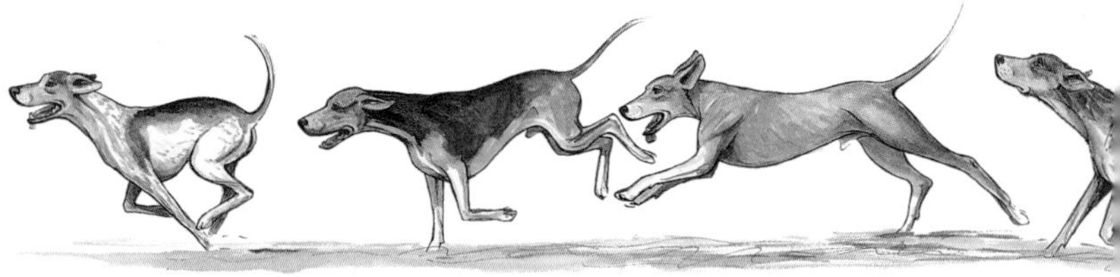

THE HUNTSMAN

The huntsman lives for his hounds. And for hunting. And for horses. But pretty much in that order. He is fond of his horses but they are, for him, more a means of transport than an end in themselves. A tool of his trade. In the same way that a passenger on a train may have an affection for the golden age of steam and Pullman dining cars and cheery porters and stations with hanging baskets but makes do with the day-to-day diesel and the processed cheese roll, the huntsman has fond memories of his great mounts of years gone by; but when the moment comes he will trade in a tired hunter and move on without a tear or a backward look.

The same is not true of his hounds. He remembers all of them. Without exception. How he bred them, whelped them, walked them. How he coupled them, old and young together, so that the new intake could learn the tricks of the trade from the old hands. Putting the headstrong young Charger with wise old Trumpet; tall, strong Brisk with the nervy but eager Tremble. Bringing out the best in the vigorous youngsters and preserving the finely wrought skills of the pack leaders. Keeping the thread. Weaving it from one generation to the next. Brighter, purer, stronger. The golden thread that binds a huntsman to his hounds and hounds to their huntsman. Such that they will seek for him, find for him, run for him till they drop and, ultimately, kill for him. And all for a kind word at the end of the day and a titbit from his pocket and for the sheer joy of it.

The huntsman has been hunting hounds for nigh on two decades and hunting to hounds for a decade before that. When he first came here the hunt was in decline with fading fields and a dwindling country. At the interview the old master asked him what he wanted from the job?

'To hunt a top pack far and wide across good country, sir!' was his response.

And what would he do to achieve that, asked the master?

The huntsman's answer secured him the job on the spot: 'Whatever it takes,' he said.

So first he began to restore the kennels. The fabric he mended with his own hard hands; cleaning, building, plastering, painting. Then he addressed the pack, using his contacts here and there to borrow, buy, breed. Introducing new blood, preserving old assets. Weaving the thread. Then he began to extend the country. Visiting the outlying farms and estates. Developing the relationships, buying the beer, collecting the fallen stock, earning respect, gaining ground. And with new ground came more and better hunting. And with better hunting came stronger, fitter hounds. And better hunts. And so the virtuous circle was squared; and the fields began to grow. Not that the huntsman gives a tinker's cuss for the field that thunders behind him across the misty sward. For him it is the hounds ahead that are everything. A dappled tan torrent in full flow and full cry. Over the hedges and across the ditches with never a check or falter from find to finish. That's hunting. Those are hounds for you. That is a huntsman.

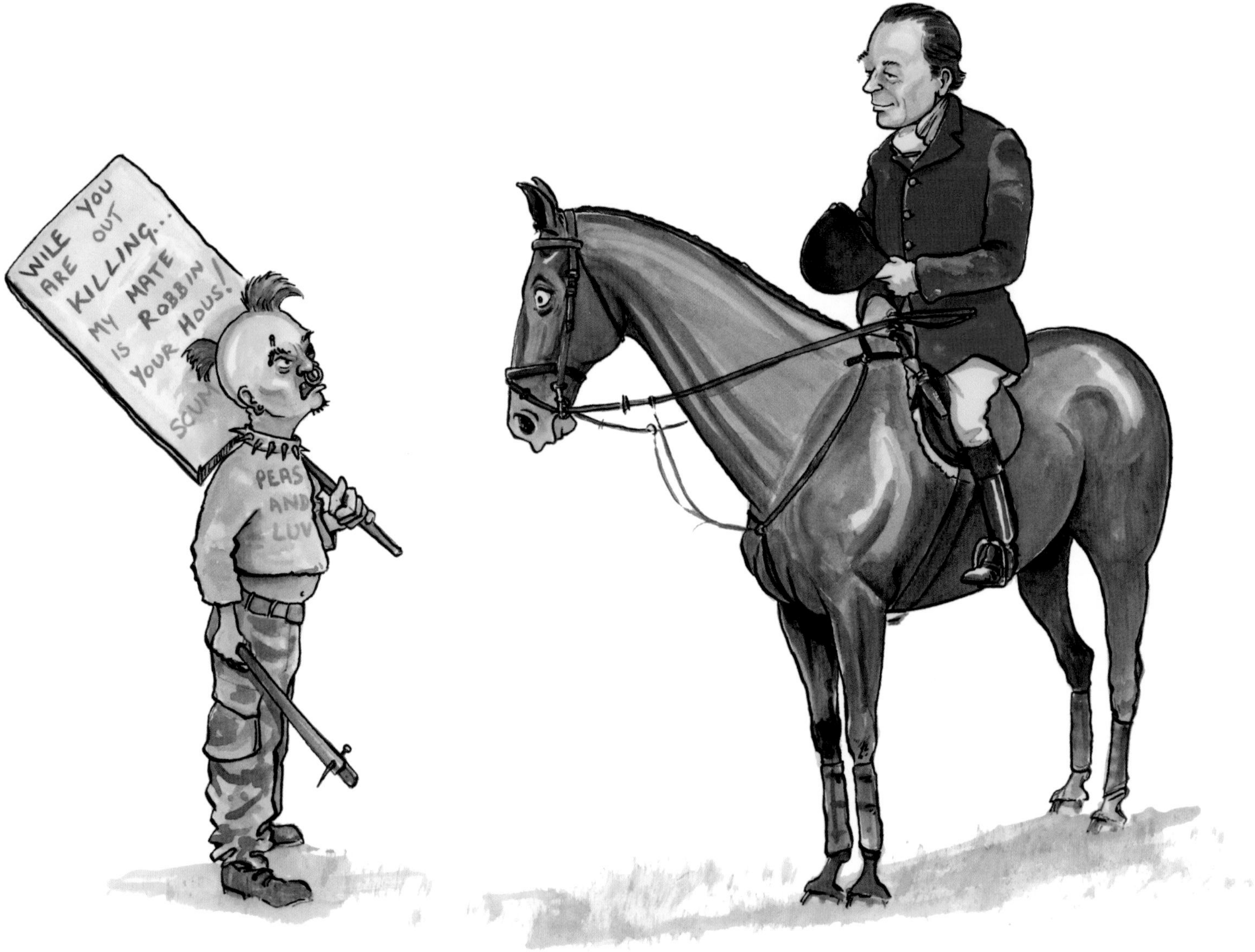
WILE YOU ARE OUT KILLING...
MY MATE IS ROBBIN YOUR HOUS!
PEAS AND LUV

Pride and Prejudice

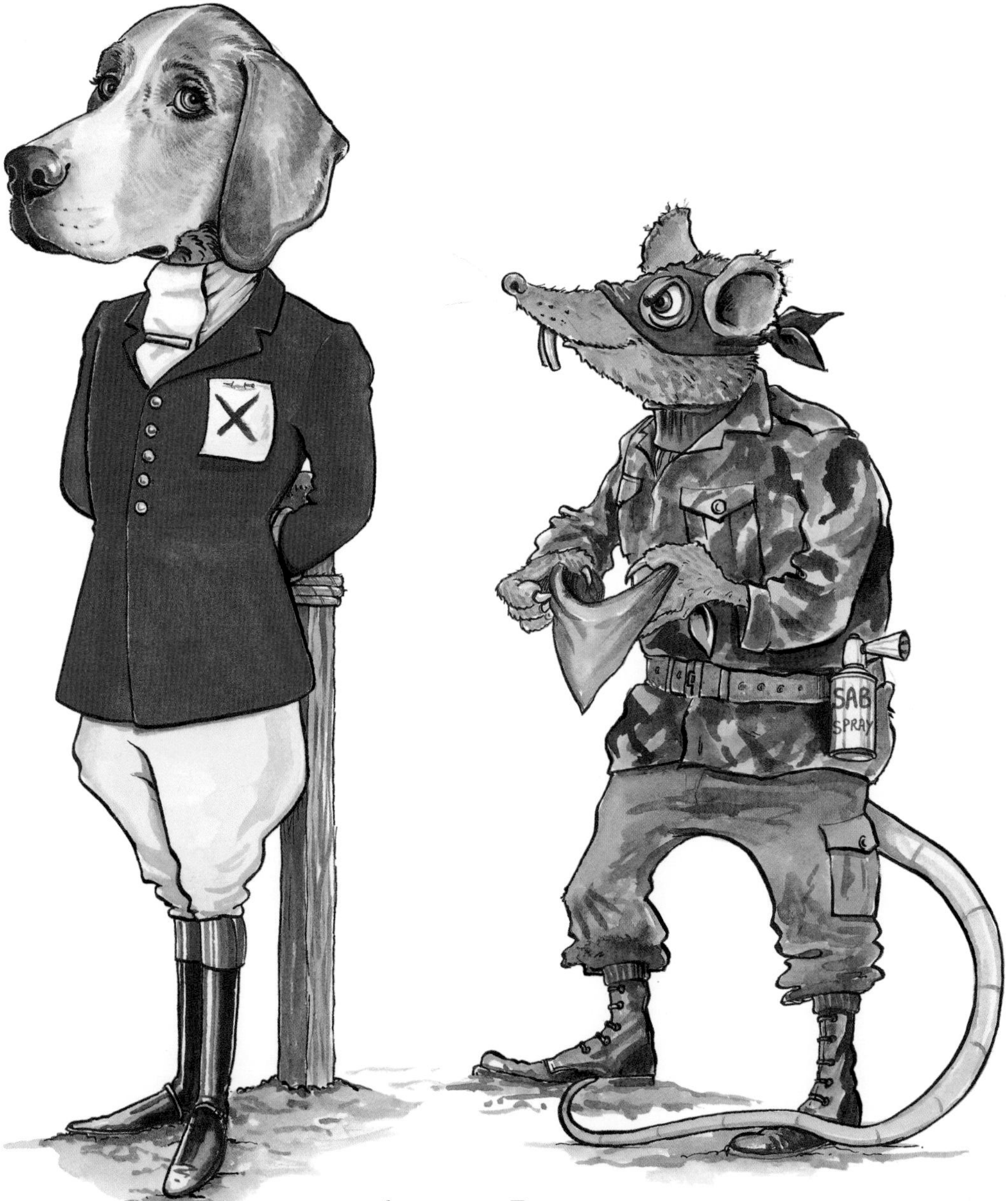
SAB
SPRAY

ANIMAL RIGHTS

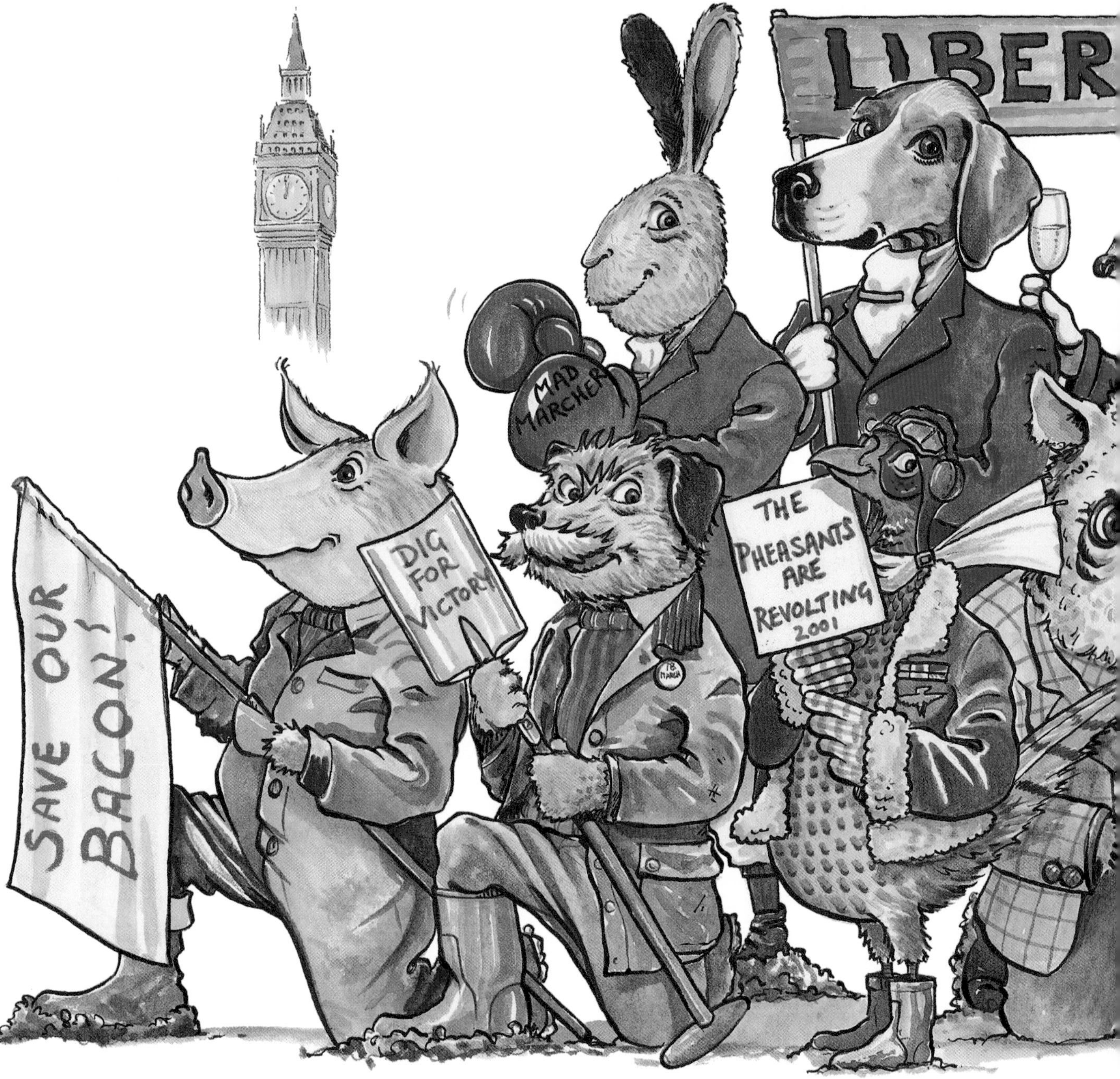
LIBER
MAD MARCHER
DIG FOR VICTORY
THE PHEASANTS ARE REVOLTING 2001
SAVE OUR BACON!

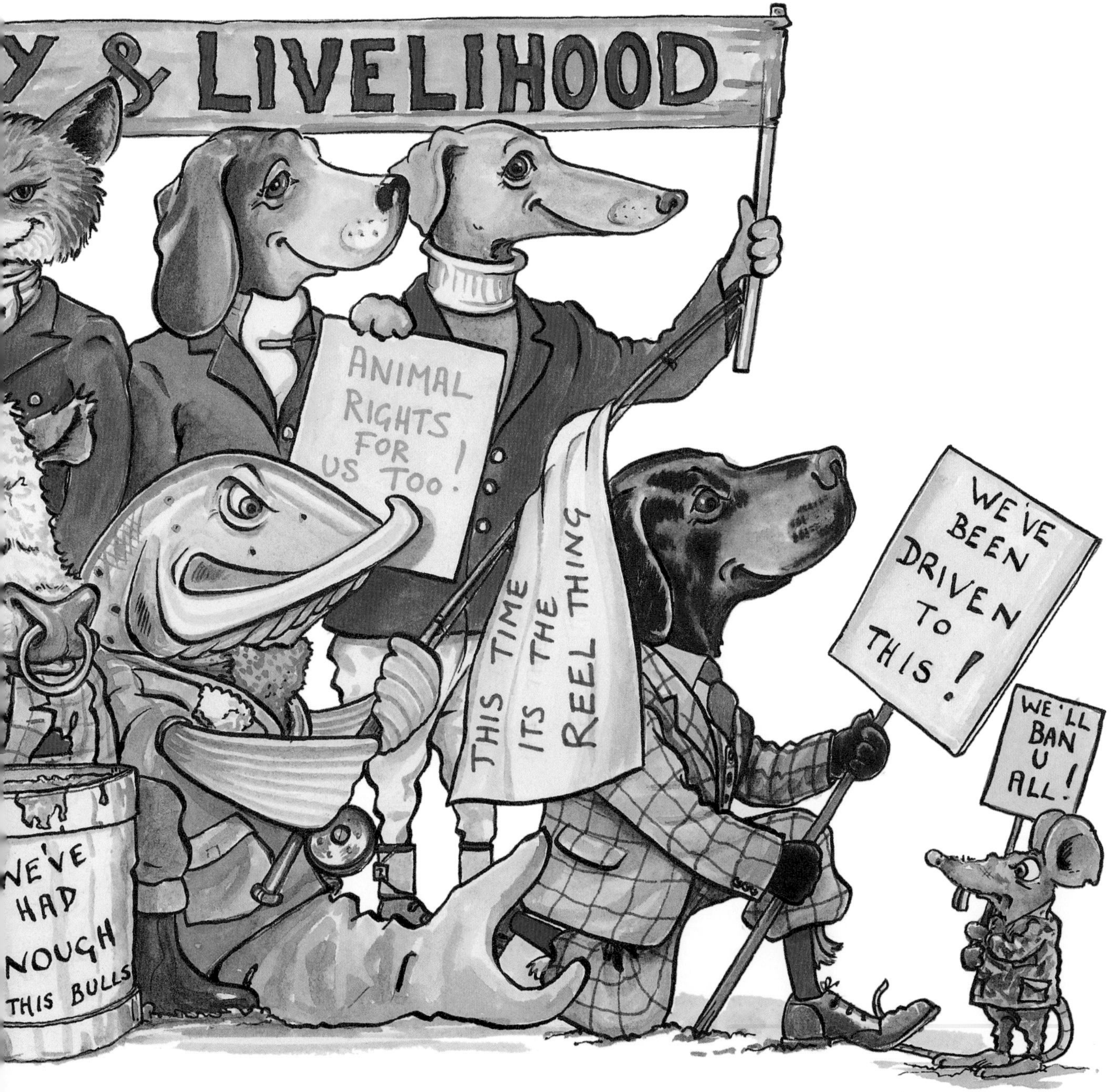
Y & LIVELIHOOD
ANIMAL RIGHTS FOR US TOO!
THIS TIME ITS THE REEL THING
WE'VE BEEN DRIVEN TO THIS!
WE'LL BAN U ALL!
E'VE HAD NOUGH THIS BULLS

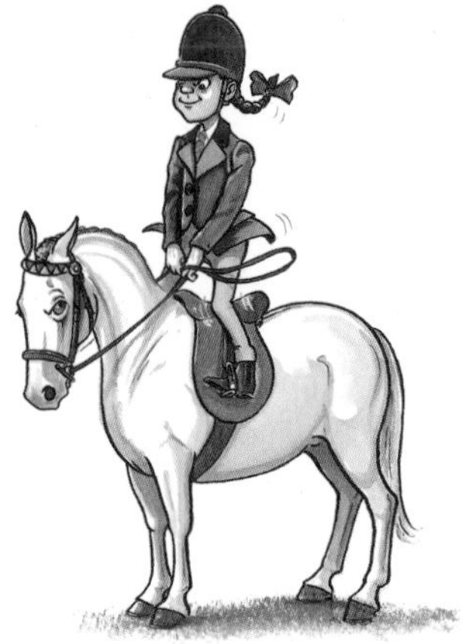
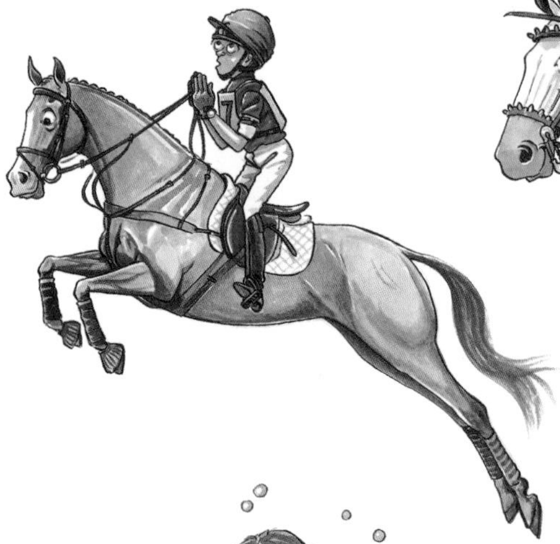
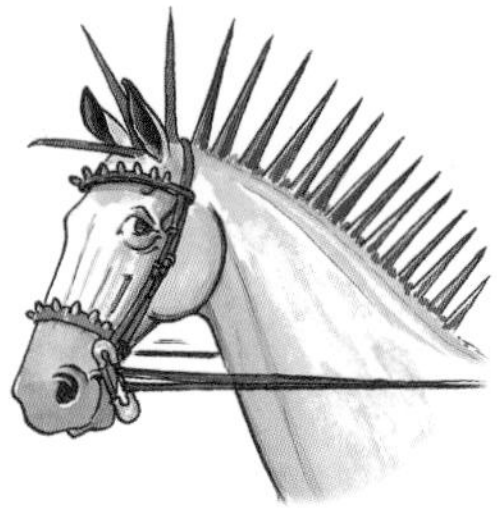
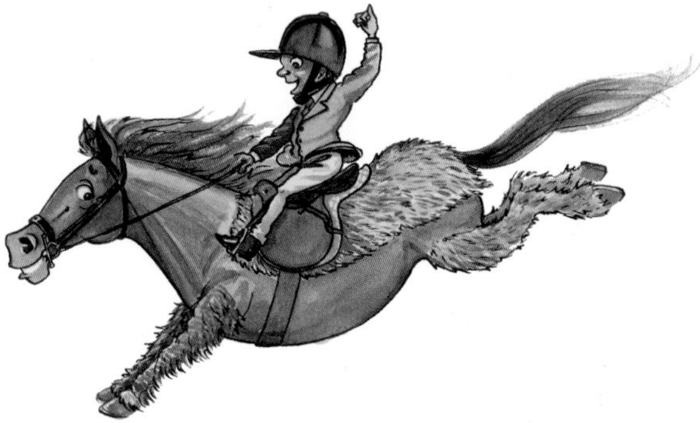
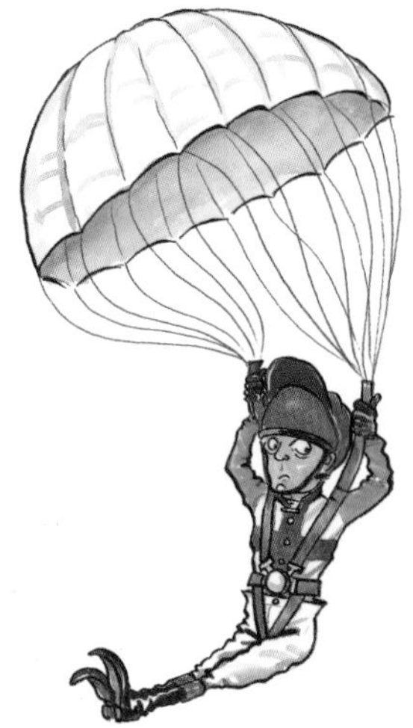
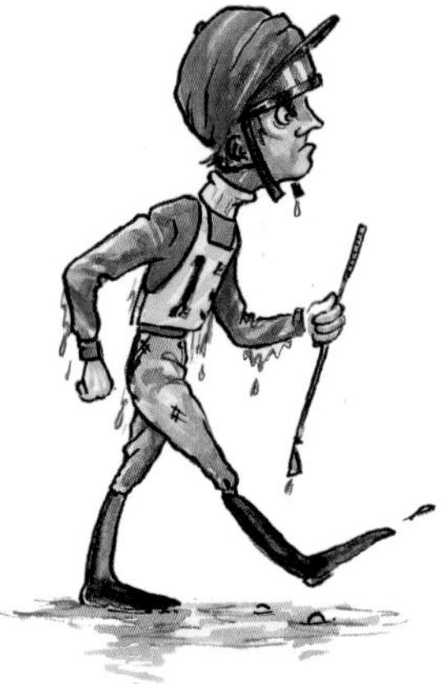
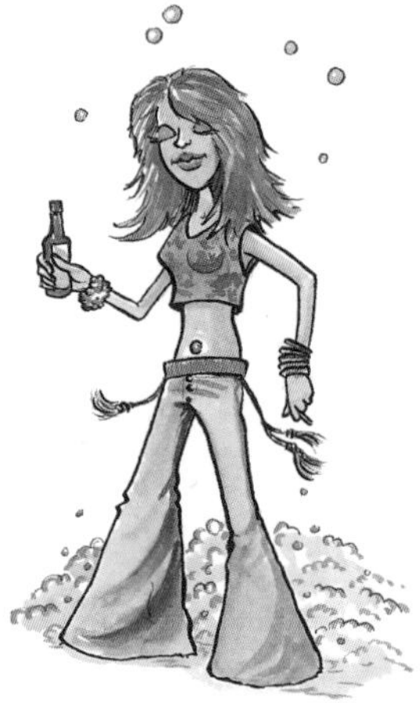
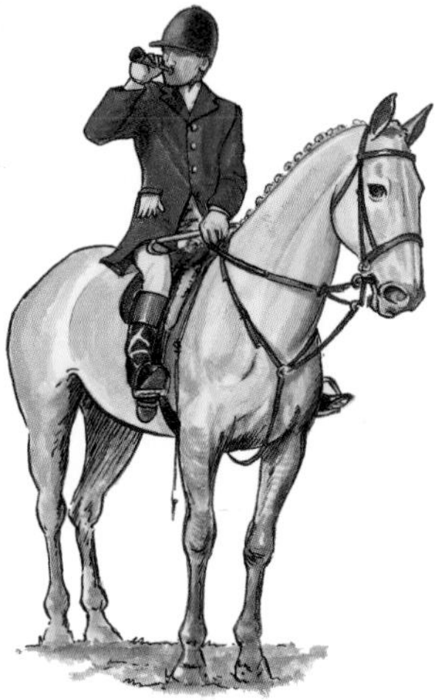
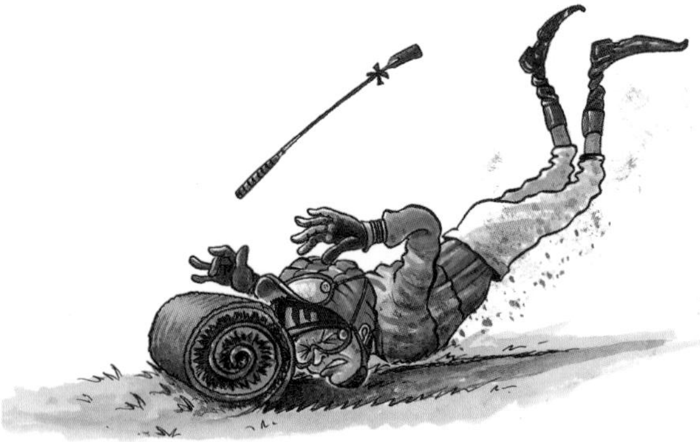
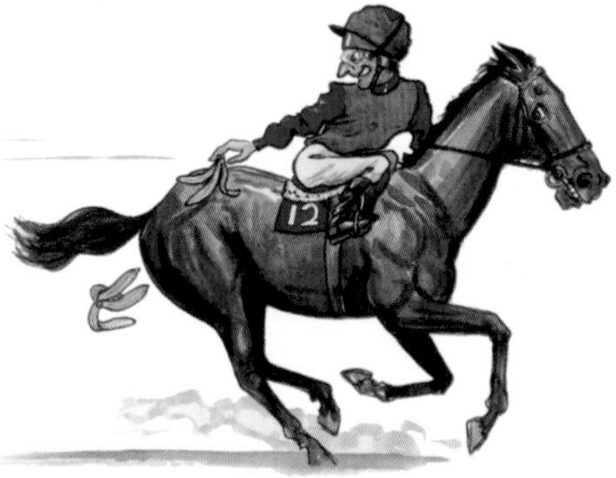
12
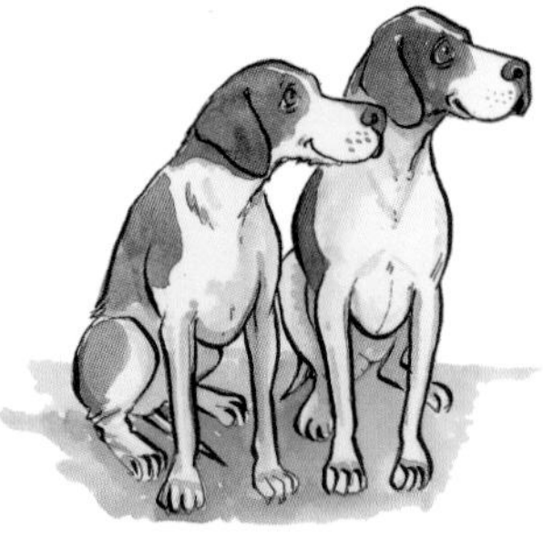